DR. JERALD BAIN

D1441460

So your child is gay

*A Guide for Canadian Families
and Their Friends*

A Phyllis Bruce Book
HarperCollins*PublishersLtd*

SO YOUR CHILD IS GAY:
A GUIDE FOR CANADIAN FAMILIES
AND THEIR FRIENDS
Copyright © 2000 by Dr. Jerald Bain.
All rights reserved. No part of this book may be
used or reproduced in any manner whatsoever
without prior written permission except in the
case of brief quotations embodied in reviews.
For information address HarperCollins
Publishers Ltd, 55 Avenue Road, Suite 2900,
Toronto, Ontario, Canada M5R 3L2.

http://www.harpercanada.com

HarperCollins books may be purchased for
educational, business, or sales promotional
use. For information please write: Special
Markets Department, HarperCollins Canada,
55 Avenue Road, Suite 2900, Toronto,
Ontario, Canada M5R 3L2.

First edition

Canadian Cataloguing in Publication Data

Bain, Jerald
So your child is gay: a guide for Canadian
families and their friends

"A Phyllis Bruce Book."
Includes bibliographical references.
ISBN 0-00-638492-7

1. Gays – Canada – Family relationships.
2. Parents of gays – Canada.
3. Parent and child.
I. Title.

HQ76.3.C3B34 2000   306.76'6
C99-932282-6

00 01 02 03 04 HC 6 5 4 3 2 1

Printed and bound in the United States

*The stories appearing in this book are drawn from actual cases but the
names and events have been altered to protect confidentiality.*

I am who I am, but you make me more with your love:

Sheila
Hilary
Zachary
Raoul
Cale

The world is full of beautiful things,
How long will man mistake it?
The folly is within ourselves,
The world is what we make it.

*The purchase
of this book was
made possible
through a generous
donation from
NOVA Corporation*

NOVA-GRACE **Women's Health**
RESOURCE LIBRARY

contents

preface *xi*

chapter 1 why this book? *1*

I DISCOVERING YOUR CHILD IS GAY

chapter 2 what to do when
           your child comes out *9*

chapter 3 the changing family *27*

II UNDERSTANDING WHY YOUR CHILD IS GAY

chapter 4 common myths
           and misconceptions *47*

chapter 5 whose life is it? *71*

chapter 6 what "causes" homosexuality? *91*

III ACCEPTING YOUR GAY CHILD

chapter 7 religious attitudes *117*

chapter 8 finding acceptance *139*

chapter 9 conclusion—for now *163*

Canadian resources *169*

bibliography *189*

index *193*

• preface

When my editor, Phyllis Bruce, and I first sat down to discuss the concept of this book, we generated many different ideas. I went off and wrote a chapter or two to give Phyllis a sense of my writing style and where I thought the book might be heading. We met again, several times and, each time, I was encouraged, Phyllis never saying anything that was negative. When I had finished the first draft, however, and saw all the notations that were sticking out of what seemed like every page, I thought: "Oh no, Phyllis has taken my book from me and rewritten it, and in the end it won't be my words, my style, my thoughts." I was wrong. Very wrong.

Phyllis Bruce is the editor's editor—professional, generous, talented. Owing to her wise counsel, the book we planned, or at least as it was formulated at our first meeting, is not the book you are about to read. I am most grateful for the respectful way in which she guided but did not censor me in the creation of this book. The responsibility for any lack of clarity, and for unorthodox, non-traditional ideas and concepts with which you might take issue, should you find them here, lies entirely with me.

The primary source of information and, I must say, inspiration came from many, many people I spoke with or interviewed.

I am especially grateful to members of the Toronto chapter of Parents, Families and Friends of Lesbians, Gays, Bisexuals and Transgenders (PFLAG). They were gracious in organizing an evening meeting at which I was able to interview some of them. That meeting set the tone for the task that lay ahead of me. Those members who provided me with their personal stories and with written material helped me clarify the approach I would take to this book.

My gratitude also goes to Esmeralda and friends, members of a Portuguese gay and lesbian community in Toronto. Their stories, courage and encouragement made a significant contribution to the way I conceived some portions of this book.

My secretary, Zahara Amaral, exhibited patience and skill beyond the call of duty as I set before her page after page, chapter after chapter, large print, fine print, all to be entered into the computer. Nothing stopped her—not even my sometimes baroque handwriting.

Finally, but not least of all, I acknowledge the devotion and patience of my family, especially my wife, Sheila, whose love and companionship have been the fundamental anchor of my life. My children never stopped giving me their support, their encouragement and their love. All of these good feelings were essential for me to be able to write the book you are now about to read.

Jerald Bain
Toronto
2000

chapter one

• why this book?

When this book was in its formative stages, a number of people asked me: why write a book that deals with the response of parents, family members and friends to the newfound knowledge that a loved one is gay or lesbian? Why, indeed?

To become a parent means to take on a multiplicity of challenges, some of them known and expected, others perhaps unanticipated. This was my experience. Who goes to parenting school? My wife and I certainly didn't. Even if we had, could our course of instruction have covered every nuance of every situation that parents face? Hardly.

Parenting is an evolutionary process that does not follow a set of rules or laws. To a large extent, you make it up as you go along. There are some basics: love, security, safety, compassion, encouragement, honesty, guidance. But even with these certainties, a child will challenge you, situations will arise which will present new, and unique, adventures in coping with the unknown.

My goal for my children was to see them develop as caring human beings equipped with the tools necessary to deal with most of the challenges and decisions that life brings. It was my hope that they would do this with creativity, with an independent spirit that would help them set and strive to achieve their own goals.

Independence—that's what I wanted for them. How shocked we are sometimes when our children actually do become independent, and their goals clash with our view of what we believe is good for them. This is the real challenge of parenting. Successful parenting is tested at many stages during a child's maturation; one of the biggest tests comes with the discovery that a child is gay or lesbian.

A parent myself, I intuitively felt that parents' understanding of their child's homosexual erotic preference would be an area of mystery, a blurry haze of confusion. My own experiences as a physician, an endocrinologist specializing in reproductive and sexual medicine, confirmed this view. I spoke not only with parents concerned about their children, but with lesbians and gays whose struggles include dealing with parents, siblings, and other family members and friends who simply cannot, or will not, understand or attempt to understand how they could be gay or lesbian, what it means to be homosexual, and what the future will bring.

My deliberations about these issues also led me to examine my own feelings, thoughts and prejudices about gays and lesbians. I asked myself some hard questions. What are my honest thoughts about homosexuality? How would I react upon discovering that one of my children was gay or lesbian? Would I be accepting or rejecting? After all, I grew up in an era of homophobia, in an era of jokes about gays. Everywhere one would turn one would find expressions of ridicule directed against homosexuals and the gay world. I had also grown up, however, in a home environment that taught me to respect the individual and that led me to question entrenched ideas. The question *Why?* became more and more a part of my thinking: Why think this way or that? Why is this the "truth" and not that? Too many times *Why?* could not be answered successfully. I had to have reasons, however, explanations for the answers to my questions; I could not accept by blind faith alone. As a consequence, dogma played a minor role in my thinking, and ultimately I concluded that there are very few absolute "truths." I hope that this book has emerged in a manner consistent with that thought process.

Several years ago, based on my own experiences as a physician, especially a physician working in a university teaching hospital and engaged in academic pursuits in addition to clinical practice, I wrote an article on the subject of parental response to the discovery that a child is gay or lesbian for a medical newspaper, *Ontario Medicine*, in which I had a regular column entitled "Sexology." That article elicited a number of responses from parents who had just discovered a child of theirs was gay or lesbian. The husband of one couple who came to see me was a physician; both husband and wife were intelligent, articulate people, who were completely taken aback by the discovery that their child was having a homosexual relationship. They didn't understand it; they didn't know to whom to turn; they didn't know how to respond; they didn't know what to do. This couple came to me because they understood that seeking assistance was appropriate; but how many thousands more would never ask for help because they were ashamed to? How many couples engage in the torturous self-analytical game of looking at "Where we went wrong?" This was a compelling reason for me to think that a book on this subject might have some meaning and be of use for a very large constituency of parents, family members and friends.

There is yet one further impetus that led me to write this book—namely, discussions I had about about this topic with patients, with groups of gays and lesbians, and with parents of homosexual children. Many communities have parent support groups, and many ideas presented in this book have arisen from interviews with members of an organization known as PFLAG (Parents, Families and Friends of Lesbians, Gays, Bisexuals and Transgenders). Participation in such groups demonstrates to parents not only that homosexuality is a common phenomenon, but that there are practical strategies for dealing with the day-to-day issues and stresses of life that parents and their homosexual children must face. Their stories are incredible and powerful. The anguish they suffered—usually needless anguish—spoke to their frustrations, misunderstandings and fears. This book is intended to assist parents, their children, and the siblings and friends who need help or information about sexuality and its variations. I hope that this book will speak not only to those who themselves are gay or lesbian or who know gays or lesbians, but to everyone who has some interest in what it means to be a human being.

This book is really about freedom—not the kind of freedom we associate with societal rights, such as freedom of assembly or freedom of the press, but personal freedom. We tend to take personal freedom for granted, and we don't generally analyse exactly what it is that we take for granted. We believe we have free will, and hence freedom of personal choice, and indeed we do, but that choice is influenced by so many factors in our lives that by the time all those factors come into play we can lose sight of the fact that we do have choices, we do have freedom. Too often, we blame these external influences rather than assuming responsibility for the choices we make.

This book asserts that human beings are the ones who interpret the world and its various perspectives, including the religious ones. This book encourages self-empowerment. We all have deliberative powers, powers of interpretation, powers of understanding, and powers to make statements or choices that don't necessarily reflect the deliberations, interpretations, understandings and choices of others.

One of the most destructive things that we human beings do is to slot others into "kinds" or "categories." We then tend to create a caricature of the category and extol its virtues or denigrate it for its misdeeds. And, further, we tend to pit one category against another, often invoking divine authority as the excuse for doing so. No human behaviour fits into a neat little package that can be sealed, labelled, and filed away. And that is true for all of us, regardless of sexual orientation.

We're all vulnerable. Education, knowledge, love, compassion, understanding, sensitivity, sympathy are far better companions in life than the injustices born of ignorance.

One final word about my subject. Some readers of this book may be upset by my omission of bisexuality. While there are individuals who engage in bisexual behavior, there is considerable controversy in the scientific community (and perhaps also in the gay, lesbian and bisexual community) about the existence of bisexual preference. Certainly we know that behavior does not always indicate preference, but may merely reflect social circumstances, such as being deprived of a sexual partner of the preferred sex. On the other hand, putting behavior aside, we know there is a clear and unequivocal distinction to be made among gays and lesbians and heterosexuals. As I do not wish to enter the debate, I do not specifically refer to bisexuality. Some will say that I have entered the controversy by not using the term "bisexual" alongside "gay" and "lesbian."

Regardless of the terminology, I hope that my message, which emphasizes the importance of individuality, personal freedom and an acceptance of diversity, is clear.

I

discovering your child is gay

• chapter two

• what to do when your child comes out

There is no one standard stereotypical family. Even the definition of family is under debate. For the purposes of this book, "family" consists of a man, a woman and a child or children. Even within that definition, there is no predictability. Each family has its own internal culture. In some families, the views of one or the other parent dominate; in others, the structure is more egalitarian. Some families view every adversity as a catastrophe; others are more amenable to change, and meet adversity with calm deliberation. Some families have a rigid belief system regarding how life should be lived; others are more laissez-faire. In some families, there is an open warm connection among the members; in others, there is cool reservation. Some husbands and wives show love and affection to each other and to the children; others either have no such feelings or if they do, will not express or demonstrate them.

Gay and lesbian children are part of all of these family configurations. There is no typical family setting in which one will find a gay child.

• *Darryl's dilemma*

Darryl, a teenager, was active, well liked, a good student and extremely attractive to girls. He often heard the boys at school talk about the girls they had successfully lured into the back of a car, or to some secluded parking spot, or to the girl's own home when her parents were away. His friends would brag about how the girl "put out", and how virile and masculine they were for coming three times with her in the space of forty-five minutes. Whether true or not, these are the stories boys tell boys. Darryl believed that he, too, should have the same experiences, so he responded to the girls' interest in him and began to have sexual interactions with some of them; often these interactions culminated in intercourse.

Darryl's sexual activity seemed fine, the right and natural thing to do, until he reached age thirty. Then he began to feel, for the first time, as if sexual intercourse with women was not necessarily the "right and natural" thing to do. If he really thought about it, he found men more sexually attractive than he did women. He was turned on by men.

It was a disturbing realization to come to. Nothing specific had happened to bring him to this new understanding; there had been no precipitating event. Had he always had this erotic feeling about men but never recognized it, thinking that "making it with girls" was what any normal teenage male would do? Now, there was no question about the intense sexual arousal he felt toward men. He no longer responded to the sexual advances of his many female friends. He needed help sorting this all out and understanding his sexuality.

Over a period of time, Darryl explored his sexual feelings in depth with the help of a psychiatrist. He not only came to understand that he was gay, but also came to accept it. And now, to tell his family.

It had never occurred to Darryl not to tell his family. He, his sister, and his parents had always been a close-knit group, able to offer one another support in times of stress or adversity. This was certainly one of those times. How would they respond? Should he even tell them? Darryl instantly knew the answer to the second question. They had always shared in each other's victories and trials. Not revealing such a significant aspect of his life would have been like living a lie, something he could not do.

How should he tell them? Darryl's family lived in a small community; he had moved away from home to go to school, and ultimately to work. Should he go home on the weekend and deliver his news in person? Should he do it by phone? He decided to do neither: he would write them a letter.

Darryl wrote the letter and sealed the envelope; he stood at the mailbox with some apprehension, then quickly dropped the envelope through the slot. The deed was done. Would the family be torn apart? He couldn't quite imagine that happening. Would they be shocked and disappointed? Would their relationship become distant and strained? Waiting for the letter to arrive was agony.

His mother called him to say "I love you." She wanted to touch and kiss him, asked him to please come home on the weekend. When he arrived home, his father greeted him with the biggest and strongest hug Darryl could ever remember receiving. His sister said, "It's nothing I didn't know for a long time. By the way, what are we going to get Mom for her birthday?"

For Darryl's family, his homosexuality was a non-issue. They fully embraced him, and they were also receptive to the gay friends that he brought home to visit. The family bond remained unshaken, and they were all able to get on with the business of living life as peacefully as possible.

Darryl knew how lucky he was. Many of Darryl's gay friends were not as fortunate; many of them were separated and alienated from their families by their lack of acceptance. How would he have coped had he suffered the same pain?

Darryl's was a warm, accepting family, but not all families have this degree of closeness and internal security. Darryl's family was concerned about itself and its own sense of well-being. Other families give much more importance to what others will think, to social status: What will our friends say? What will the community think? How can we face the people we know without feeling a sense of shame? Families with confidence and acceptance can deal with this aspect much more readily.

There are many challenges to face when a child comes out; personal acceptance is one, and dealing with others outside the immediate family circle is another. The ways in which these sensitive areas are handled will have a significant impact on your child and your relationship with him or her.

• the "perfect" family

Eugene and Helen were a picture-perfect couple with a picture-perfect family. Eugene was a successful dentist, driving the "right" car and living in the "right" neighborhood. Helen, an artist, made a handsome living as an interior designer. They were very much in love; they were very compatible, viewing life in a similar way and striving for the same goals. They were sexually attracted to each other and expressed their shared passion often. They had three daughters, each of them beautiful, intelligent, talented, creative. Life was ideal; Eugene and Helen had everything. That was three years ago.

Elise, their eldest, had been a high-school cheerleader, the prom-queen type. The phone had never stopped ringing. It seemed as if every boy at school was drawn to her. It wasn't hard to understand: she was vivacious, bright and alive. But Elise wasn't interested in them.

At first, Eugene and Helen thought that she was too absorbed in her studies, and in her extracurricular activities, to respond to every advance by every young man who tried to enter her life. But if she was so absorbed in her many pursuits, why did she have time to talk with the girls who called, and why was she now going out only with girls?

Helen tried in different ways to engage Elise in conversations about her social life. Why was she so short with the boys and so elusive? Elise became defensive: "Why do you ask so many questions? It's my life and I'll lead it the way I want to."

Family life became somewhat strained. Helen tried to learn about Elise's private life through her two other daughters, both younger than Elise. They were quite protective of their sister and requested that their mother not ask so many questions and not worry so much. Elise is just fine, they told her; don't be a smothering mother.

Helen didn't think she was smothering; she thought she was simply looking out for her child's best interests and, to do that, had to know if there was anything troubling her. If she was being so evasive and so secretive, then there surely must be something troubling her.

Finally, Elise felt she could encourage the charade no longer.

She sat down with Eugene and Helen and told them what Helen had feared all along. She was sexually and emotionally attracted to women. She used the word "lesbian." Eugene and Helen sat in stunned silence, and tears filled Helen's eyes. Instinctively they knew they would never reject their daughter, but at that moment they felt paralyzed, unable to reach out to her.

"Are you sure?"

"Yes, Mom, I'm sure."

"How do you know?"

"Dad, I know. I have a lover and I know."

Eugene and Helen's world had just come apart. Helen sat in seclusion in the study for days after that. Eugene went to work but functioned like an automaton. Days and weeks passed, and the family gradually shook off its lethargy. Elise moved in with her lover and thrived, but Eugene and Helen could simply not regain that lust for life they had once displayed.

Helen lost her interest in sexual activity and now began to say no to Eugene's advances. Their world—their hopes, expectations and dreams—had been shattered.

• a lost son

The tragic story of Don, written by his mother, Eunice, received prominence in a national newspaper. Don had died more than twenty years earlier. Eunice's faith dictated that Don had died because of sins committed. But who was to accept blame for these sins? Eunice asked for an answer. Many who read the newspaper article would wonder why she had to ask. Wasn't the answer obvious? Many readers believed it was, though not all of them would point to the same answer.

Don excelled at school; he was clearly much more academically and intellectually endowed than his siblings. He handled high school, and university, with relative ease; he was devoted to his studies, because he knew that a good education would help ensure his future.

Soon after his father's death, Don gathered the courage to inform his mother that he was gay. He felt intuitively that he could never have told his father, who would have reacted harshly. Don, however, was not prepared for his mother's response. Eunice was shocked by his news. She did not look at Don as her son, her flesh and blood whom she had nursed and nurtured. She did not look into her own heart for compassion. She believed with all her heart that her faith superseded her familial and genetic link with Don. She believed that her own anguish took precedence over that of her son.

Eunice turned to her faith because she believed she had nowhere else to turn and that no other source of guidance was reliable. Her faith could not be wrong.

Her faith, she decided, was the rock upon which she could stand unswervingly in order to undertake three courses of action. The first was to urge Don to go for psychiatric therapy. He could only respond with a look of sadness. The second was to implore him to fall on his knees in prayer, begging for salvation. The third course of action she almost immediately put into effect.

She brought her other children together for a family meeting without Don. She told them that Don was gay and that there was only one appropriate response to this situation, according to their faith: Don must be ignored, shunned, until he saw the error of his ways and recanted. This family policy was acted upon immediately.

Don was completely ignored by his family for the better part of a year. He had lost his most valued possession, the love and support of his family. If he had not come out to his family he would have betrayed himself; but, to his family, his actions seemed to have betrayed them. As strong as Don was, any strength he might have had to withstand the rejection by his family had been completely sapped. Death by his own hand was the only way that Don could deal with his depression.

Eunice subscribed to a belief system that categorizes human behavior according to rigid rules of correctness. Does she still adhere to this faith? Has she interpreted her faith correctly? How does her faith explain this tragedy?

And what of Don's siblings? Perhaps one day they'll write their stories or somehow tell us what they felt, what they experienced. Perhaps not. Do they face the questions their mother does? Is their faith ever-strong, unshaken, unshakable? Or do they suffer a silent pain that only time or a therapeutic intervention can help to ease? We'll likely never know.

Don's story is an extreme one. Fortunately, his story is not typical, but, then, is there a "typical" story? Likely not. Each story is unique.

• what is your family like?

Everyone who is reading these stories is in a family or at least came out of a family of one sort or another. Perhaps your family is like Darryl's—kind and tolerant. Perhaps it is like Elise's—unable to accept. Perhaps it is like Don's—rigid and unforgiving. Discovering that your child's sexuality is not necessarily what you expected it to be or wanted it to be can be a surprise, even shattering. Although there are many influences you can exert over your child, you have absolutely no control over his or her sexual orientation. That is something which is exclusively part of his or her being. Accepting that concept will make it easier for you to accept your child, and the open expression of his or her erotic preference.

Darryl's family was almost matter-of-fact about his coming out. They adopted the attitude "Okay. That's interesting, but, so what?" They gave Darryl love and respect, as part of getting on with living. This is an exceptional response, and it underlines the basic security within the family, and the confidence family members have as a unit. The outside world, if it presents a problem, would have to adjust to this family, and not the other way around.

Elise, on the other hand, came from a family whose strength depended so much on the expectations that were placed on the children and on what the outside world thought of them. They had always done the "right" things, lived in the "right" neighborhoods, had their proper place in the "right" social circles. Sensing that it was not "right" to have a homosexual child, they felt alienated.

Don's family was the extreme of rigidity and orthodoxy, allowing absolutely no room to maneuver. There was no discussion. There was no acceptance. There was not even a crack in the door of understanding. This is a tragic, unforgiving family that will continue to suffer in solitude unless it can break the silence in a meaningful way.

Everyone reading this book, by virtue of being a human being, has a sexual orientation that is usually (but not invariably) exclusively directed toward one sex or another. We each identify ourselves as heterosexual or homosexual or bisexual, and, for the most part, our sexual behavior generally reflects our sexual orientation.

The most common mode of sexual living is heterosexual. The most prevalent family structure is a heterosexual man living with a heterosexual woman. We know, however, that sometimes appearances can be misleading. Gay men do marry straight women and have children; lesbian women do marry straight men and have children. But in most cases, the family unit is heterosexual, for both the couple and the children they bear.

How do you respond, then, upon learning that a family member, particularly a child, is gay or lesbian? At some time in the distant future, this may be a trite or naive question; someday one's sexual orientation may be irrelevant to friends, family and society, because individuals will no longer be distinguished on the basis of sexual orientation. But we don't live in that idyllic time yet. We live in the cold, hard realities of today.

Homosexuality does not stand in full equality with heterosexuality in our world. Society doesn't welcome gays and lesbians into its warm embrace the way it welcomes heterosexual individuals and couples. Parents in a heterosexual marriage expect their children will be like them—heterosexual. Anything else is either a surprise or a shock or a sin.

In today's reality, our question remains: A family member declares himself gay or declares herself lesbian—how do you respond? To answer, step outside of yourself for a moment and try to visualize yourself as the person who has just declared his or her homosexuality. As that person, you are in a state of apprehension—you can't be sure how your mother, father, sister, brother, aunts, uncles, cousins or friends are going to respond. Will they reject you? Will they embrace you? Will they be stunned into silence?

You are about to declare something about yourself that doesn't quite fit into society's expectations of how a life should be led. Being "different" raises fears and anxieties. And what about all those "normal" things society expects of us: a traditional relationship, children, adherence to a particular code of behavior. All those expectations are about to be shattered.

But *is* the gay or lesbian person really all that "different"? Are you creating imaginary differences to somehow justify placing yourself in opposition to the declared sexual orientation of your child or family member?

Most people, especially those whose family environment is reasonably comfortable, want to tell family members about important aspects of their lives. We all want to share the happy moments that we experience—moments of joy, moments of pride: our success at school, our promotion on the job, the purchase of something significant, the vacation we're about to take, and so much more. We also want to share the sad moments as we look for solace, for comfort, for reassurance. And then there are moments that are neither happy nor sad, but are of special significance to us. We often turn to family members to help us make decisions, to help us see the pros and cons of a particular issue, the up side and the down side, the whole dimension rather than just the narrow or one-sided view we often adopt because we really want it to be that way.

Sexual orientation is certainly a major fact of life. Heterosexual individuals, however, don't agonize over how to tell family members, or anyone else for that matter, about their heterosexuality. They usually don't have to announce things that are expected or taken for granted.

Homosexuality is a surprise, something unexpected, something that is misunderstood and too often disdained. This mainstream view of homosexuality is so pervasive that, to some extent, it is manifest in the homosexual individual him- or herself. Imagine the questions that run through the mind of a gay or lesbian who is dealing with the issue of disclosure: Shall I tell? Whom shall I tell? How shall I tell it? What will be the response? Will I be ridiculed or condemned? Will I be embraced? Will I be ignored, ostracized, excommunicated? Whatever I do, things will be different, won't they?

Gay men and lesbians want to come out to their families. Not doing so means living a lie, a masquerade. And they want their families, at the very least, to be respectful of them, even if they can't be totally accepting. The family may never completely understand, but understanding is not a prerequisite for love and acceptance.

• Carlo's story

One of the most moving family stories I know is the story of Carlo, who immigrated from a distant country, leaving behind his entire family: mother, father, brother, sister, brother-in-law, nieces and nephews.

The macho-male tradition was very strong in Carlo's home country. Somewhere around age twelve, Carlo remembers being uncomfortable with his sexuality. He was confused, unsure of himself. He denied his sexual feelings—as he said, "I didn't want to be gay". He kept all these feelings and thoughts about his uncertainty toward his sexual expression within himself.

By age twenty-two, Carlo's discomfort had become intolerable; he had to speak to someone. He sought help from a psychologist, not knowing how he would be received, whether he would emerge from counseling feeling better or worse. Fortunately he found a counselor who understood that it was much more important to focus on Carlo's anxiety and distress than on his homosexuality. He was, after all, homosexual; this was clear. His anxiety, on the other hand, was something to be treated, something that was subject to change.

Carlo emerged from therapy a different person. In acknowledging and accepting his homosexuality, he had gained self-assurance and now understood that he was a whole person. He had regained his self-esteem. With this total acceptance of himself, Carlo was now able to get on with his life.

Carlo had recently graduated from university. He knew he had to gather his thoughts about his career, about where he wanted to live, about when and how to tell his family he was gay. Fortunately, he had options he could consider. He came to the realization that he could make no significant decisions in his home environment. He must move, not just to another city, but to another culture, to a totally different environment. His family understood this and supported his move, believing, of course, that he would soon be convinced that there was no place like home.

Carlo moved to a large cosmopolitan city, a meeting place of the world's nations, the world's cultures, the world's variations in sexual orientation. He came to understand that homosexuality was common. Not only was he not alone, both as a new immigrant and as a gay man, but he soon found soul mates, and even a special friend and companion. Carlo had left a warm and embracing family. He had always shared all aspects of his life with his family. He realized that he must now share his most painful secret with them. He wanted his family to know who he truly was, and not just who they believed he was.

Here is the letter that Carlo sent to his family:

To my dearest family,

I am writing you the most important letter of my life. And I do it now because I feel you so close to my heart, even though we're so far apart. It's because I feel that you love me so, and because I feel that I love you so, that I have to tell you the truth about me. How do you think I am? I am everything you know about me, what each and every one of you knows about me plus a very important part that I am now revealing: I am a man who is capable of loving another man, i.e., I'm gay. I'm sorry if I shock you. Maybe the fact that I didn't accept my own sexuality for so many years shaped my personality; but who I am and how you know me, that didn't change. What changed or will change is your attitude towards me, just like my own changed, opening a new way in the search of happiness—my happiness. Believe me, this is not a choice. It would be a lot easier for me to be heterosexual. I just needed to be honest to myself and to you. And if this is the reality, why should I lie—just because of what other people might think? Nobody chose to be heterosexual, right? Well, I didn't choose to be homosexual either, and if this is the way I am, what I am going to do is to look for someone to love and to relate to according to what I believe to be worth it: feelings. Could you imagine what it was like to live with such a strong homophobia inside me? It was pushing me into the erasure of my life, by erasing my sexuality. But I couldn't do it because this type of sexuality exists in 10 percent of all men and women, just like there's a percentage of that population who is left-handed or has eyes of a particular color. The conceptions that our society forces us to accept drag us into condemnation and prejudice. But I am not just my sexuality and I don't want to be judged upon it. My sexuality is only a significant part of who I am. I am not asking for your understanding. Nobody wants to understand why you're left-handed or six feet tall. You simply accept that that's the way that person is. I only ask you to write me back telling me what you think, but most of all how you feel. It would be unfair for all of us if I didn't tell you this . . . because I was being incomplete. I know that I am risking everything from this letter on, but you are who I most care about and it is you who I will always keep in my heart, no matter what. Only now I am the true Carlo to you but always the same as your son, brother, brother-in-law and uncle.

Carlo

His mother, sister and brother all responded. First, the letter from his mother:

Dear Carlo,

I received your letter yesterday and I'm still trying to deal with it. Although it is a reality that is yours and that I respect, I have to tell you that I was shocked. But I am confronting it and I'm doing it alone. Since you opened your heart, why don't you tell me more about it, how and when it started, if you were spontaneously attracted or not, etc. Wouldn't you like to be a father? To have your own children? The way you love children . . . knowing how affectionate you are, please don't give yourself too much to someone and please be careful. Worse than anything would be finding out that you were sick, if you know what I mean. Apart from the shock (I know I shouldn't be), this doesn't change at all the love that I feel for my dear son. Nobody is perfect. By the way, tell me: is homosexuality genetic or not? There are different opinions, but do you think that you were born like that or the circumstances and the way we brought you up? Please be careful and live your happiness your own way, and I want you to know that you can always count on your mother's understanding and lots and lots of love.

I miss you very much. Accept a very tight hug from your mother always.

This letter comes from a mother who has unconditional love in her heart for her son. This is a letter written with love, respect and concern. Carlo's mother raises natural questions: Was it the way your father and I raised you that made you gay? Do we pass it on to you through our genes? Please be careful and not get "sick" (presumably she is worried about AIDS). Even though she is concerned, as any mother would be, for Carlo's mother love and support are primary: "You can always count on your mother's understanding and lots and lots of love. I miss you very much. Accept a very tight hug from your mother, always."

His sister also responded:

> Carlo,
>
> I accept you as you are, my dear youngest brother, and at the same time my oldest, that listens to me and gives me advice, my friend. I feel sorry for this, but what hurts me more is the fact that you suffered for so long. Have you ever had a boyfriend? Don't you think it's weird two men kissing each other? Well, if it wasn't the case with someone so close we would probably still be making jokes about gay people; now, we have to think twice. And if somebody asks me if you have a girlfriend, what should I say? Please don't be afraid to talk about it, tell me if you have a boyfriend or not, if you were dumped, etc. I want to let you know that you will always be my dearest brother who I really love very much and miss so much that I cry for. You will always be my dearest brother whatever your option is, and a beautiful uncle because we will always love you. Many kisses from your sister that adores you.

The final letter was from Carlo's brother:

> Why didn't you tell me before? Maybe I offended you so many times . . . I apologize to you because I didn't know. You don't have to be afraid of anything; you just have to be who you are, true. The love I feel for you doesn't change—quite the opposite. You deserve everything and you have to be happy. And I wish you this as much as I wish it for my daughter. I never thought I would say

these words in my life, but since it is the reality we have to live with it. I respect your decision and I don't want you to suffer, I always want you to be happy and alive, feeling good with who you are, because if you feel good, so will we. We've always been a very close family and we won't stop being one because of your letter. You are always welcome to my house. So this is how I feel about this situation; I wrote this letter from the bottom of my heart and not just to please you or make you happy. So you know that you can always count on my support no matter what happens. A big hug from a brother who loves you so much just the way you are.

How lucky Carlo is to have such a warm, sympathetic, expressive and intelligent family. How lucky the family is to have Carlo. Life for Carlo, as a gay man, will have challenges, but the unconditional love and support of his family will be a tremendous buffer against any adversities he may face.

• chapter three

• the changing family

When, as parents we learn that a child is gay or lesbian, is our distress really a manifestation of our concern over what effect this fact will have on our identity, our life? Are we concerned about what the rest of the family, and our friends and neighbors, will think? About what pattern of recriminations we will fall into? What alienation or derision we will suffer? What deprivations we will endure—the loss of a hope for grandchildren, and of the family environment we believed would be ours forever?

These are natural feelings and there's no shame in having them or in expressing them openly. When you are troubled, do you keep it to yourself or do you find a sympathetic ear and share your tale of woe, or bitterness, or concern?

Here is the answer of one mother, Barbara. I met Barbara at a meeting of PFLAG (Parents, Families and Friends of Lesbians, Gays, Bisexuals and Transgenders) I attended, hoping to discuss the book I was about to write and to hear how different families dealt with a child's coming out as gay or lesbian. After Barbara's son came out, she began to read about lesbian and gay experience. She also began to write, putting down her thoughts and feelings into short essays that captured a particular emotion or idea. Most of her writings were meant for her own private reflection. I'm grateful to Barbara for allowing me to use one of them in this book.

A Plea to Parents—Please Reach Out and Listen

I had very little knowledge of gays and lesbians. These were only words in the press and I must admit I never perused those articles. I wasn't interested.

I now have a folder (affectionately known within our family as the "G" file). It is expanding weekly!

I am very interested in acquiring information and thus knowledge of gays and lesbians and of a particular group known as PFLAG. Yes, my world has changed and I began to open my eyes and my heart. I am learning and growing. Do you wonder the reason for this dramatic reversal? My son is gay. He knew for several months before he shared his "secret" with me. As a stay-at-home, hands-on parent, I was suddenly faced with an unsolvable confrontation. I was unable to change these words that I was hearing.

My son would not be marrying a young lady who would be my daughter-in-law. All of a sudden in a flash, the grandchildren that I had desired became a thought of the past. And yes, many gays and lesbians do now have children, but my son says that he will not subject a child to the ridicule, teasing and discrimination that he realizes is now a part of his life. (But maybe we as a society can change that.)

My son hasn't changed. He is still my wonderful, caring and sensitive friend. We have always shared a very special relationship and that will, of course, continue. But instead of a daughter-in-law, I will be embracing another son whom I will feel fortunate to know and love.

And that is the reason that my "G" file is growing. I must learn, so that I can educate others. Parents reading this article might one day hear the words that will alter their lives and change the dreams that they as parents had for their children: "I can't believe that I am telling you this: I am gay."

We must help these young people. They must not be left to struggle alone; too many face an insurmountable future.

I was lucky; my son felt secure enough to share his discovery with me. But many young people don't follow a similar route. You will read the details in the newspaper—no, not in the sports or entertainment sections. As horrifying as it sounds, the obituary column attests to the fact that many teens or young adults feel there is no family or society acceptance and understanding. These young people exit this world in the prime of their lives. And often their families never do know the real reason for their children's despair and suicides. Please listen and reach out to your children. They are a product of you—their parents. Do not desert them! This is not a chosen lifestyle.

PFLAG is an association of parents/families and friends of lesbians and gays. They are caring people reaching out to others. They will help you. Please give PFLAG and your children the attention that they deserve. I know, because I am a new member and they were there for me.

• family strength

When we are troubled or there's something on our minds, where do we turn? Often we keep these disturbing thoughts to ourselves, hoping either that the problem will go away or that we will find the solution on our own. For short-term problems, this is often a very successful approach. This is the strategy that most of us try as a first step if the challenge we face has a limited life span. But when the problem is not transitory, often we grow even more anxious if we don't talk to someone, either simply to lighten the burden, or to get advice or guidance on managing or dealing with the problem.

The person we turn to may be a friend or a family member. Sometimes the person we turn to is our doctor or lawyer or accountant. Whom we select depends on the nature of the problem. The family, however, is usually the most solid foundation we have. It is the family's warmth, support and understanding that give us the greatest hope, the strongest resolve to do what we have to do in order to confront whatever troubles us. We hope the family will listen and understand. After all, isn't that what families are for?

Imagine, then, what it's like for a gay or lesbian child who wants to share his or her life with the family but is in anguish over whether to disclose his or her homosexuality, perhaps because of the shocked response it might induce, or because of the family's religious beliefs, or because homophobia has been openly expressed within the family. The greatest fear of all may be the fear of abandonment.

Nurturing parents prepare their children for a life of self-identity and self-sufficiency, which means that they are equipped ultimately to leave home and carve out an independent life. Children take to independence quite readily because the expression of individual freedom is a natural part of being human. But children from an emotionally nurturing background don't take their individual freedom to mean separation and alienation from their family. They take it to mean self-sufficiency, self-identity but with a foundation in and a connection to the family that nurtured them. No matter how strong the spirit of independence is, connection to family remains a powerful force, and abandonment a crushing blow.

Study after study has shown one consistent fact: there is a tremendous buffering effect on stress when we can discuss our problems with family members. Family members have significantly more in common than even the best of friends do. You share roots, a history, a past with the family, a unique and fortifying fact of existence. To lose this connection both from the point of view of the individual and of the family as a whole, is to lose a part of your essential being. Both the rejected individual and the rejecting family member lose.

Children withhold lots of personal information, but when it comes to the really big things in life, it's hard not to tell parents, because disclosure removes the stigma of deceit. Children also want the blessings of their parents in the things that they do, in the person that they are. The most potent approval is parental approval. It provides solace, consolation and fortification against the adversities of the world, of everyday life.

Talking about life's stresses with another person, especially life-altering stresses, provides an important shield against the psychological effects brought on by that stress. The more important the person you talk to is in your life, the stronger the buffering effect. For most young people, parents are the most significant "others." The family, both the individual members and as a totality, relieves stress by providing validation, love and comfort. How deprived is that family whose interpersonal relationships are distant or virtually non-existent.

If a child hides his or her homosexuality behind the mask of heterosexuality, there are many consequences: isolation, alienation, loss of self-confidence and self-esteem. The child lives a lie, which increases stress, diminishes self-concept and decreases self-acceptance. It creates a gulf between self and family. How can anyone feel normal or happy under these circumstances?

Studies have shown that three out of four homosexuals maintain a heterosexual front. If self-disclosure is the primary determinant of intimacy, can you imagine what a tremendous emotional and psychological burden it must be for someone to put up a heterosexual facade in the presence of a gay or lesbian reality?

In her doctoral thesis on the coming-out process, Karen Kaffko, Department of Social Work, York University, Toronto, listed a number of reasons why homosexuals do not disclose their sexual orientation: they fear rejection, their parents would suffer psychically, the offspring would feel guilty, they fear being forced to go to therapy, they are uncertain about their own sexual identity, sex is not discussed in the family, the family has too many other problems. Kaffko also identifies some of the reasons why people do come out to their families: they hope that disclosure will reduce the costs associated with pretending; they want to open up communication within the family; they want to strengthen family bonds, deepen love, provide opportunities for mutual support and caring; they want to feel better about themselves.

Gays and lesbians who have not yet come out feel a sense of restriction and inhibition, a sense of not being themselves. Disclosure, especially to the family, provides a profound sense of liberation, of freedom, of being allowed to be yourself in an open, uninhibited fashion. The pain of pretence vanishes.

• Emily's secret

Emily experienced the stifling, smothering sensation of living a lie and not being able to be herself.

Emily first became aware of having feelings for other females when she was about fifteen years old. These feelings weren't necessarily sexual in nature, but they were feelings of attraction, of an affinity, that she could not clearly express. She heard a radio program discussing homosexuality. She recognized and identified with many facets of the discussion, and she wondered whether she, in fact, might be homosexual. Although she was always a very animated person, she recalls that her teen years were dark and depressing. Emily was in pain, not only because she felt she couldn't expose what she now recognized as her lesbianism, but also because she thought she was an aberration. There were relatively few other lesbians around and certainly none within her sphere of activity.

She was quite surprised, however, and reassured, when she discovered that some of her schoolmates had also borrowed the book on homosexuality that she had taken out of the school library. She found their names on the book's lending card. This gave her considerable relief. She now felt she had to explore the true nature of her sexual state.

At age twenty she had sexual intercourse with a man for the first time. This man became her boyfriend, not so much from the sexual perspective, but from the point of view of being her soul mate. Both Emily's parents were emotionally abusive toward her (her mother had also been physically abusive) and in her boyfriend, Emily found a safe and comforting haven, someone with whom she could share most of the significant parts of her life (except her feelings toward women)

Despite the care, attention and support Emily received from her boyfriend, she wanted more and more to be with a woman. She was quite desperate in her feelings of isolation. These feelings were heightened when, after a terrible argument with her father, during which he almost choked her, she decided she could no longer live at her parents' home. She discussed all of this with her boyfriend—even the fact that she suspected she was lesbian. She became depressed, even suicidal, and throughout all of this her boyfriend supported her.

She needed a female companion—not simply for sexual activity, but for understanding and validation. Finally, at the university she was attending, she discovered and joined a lesbian support group. This was what she was after; her suicidal ideas disappeared; her depression left her. She knew now, without question, that she was a lesbian. Her self-esteem rose, and she even became a facilitator and role model in her university women's support group. Despite all the emotionally suppressive experiences she had suffered because of parental abuse, she felt that she could not live a lie with her parents. They had to know.

She first disclosed to her sister. Her sister's response: "I know that." Nevertheless, her sister had a difficult time dealing with Emily's information and offering her the warmth that she needed. Emily then telephoned her brother and came out to him. Immediately upon hanging up the phone, he came over to her apartment, gave her a big hug and told her he loved her.

Now, to tell her parents. It was Christmas Eve; perhaps not the ideal time, but her mother was ill in bed, and when Emily came to visit, her mother asked about her boyfriend. As unplanned as it was, this was the moment to disclose: "Mom, I'm a lesbian."

Her mother started crying uncontrollably. "How could you do this to me? You could destroy your life."

When her mother calmed down a bit, Emily seized the moment. She told her mother things that had been in her heart for years—about the pain of her youth, about the abuse, about the ridicule she received from her father in deciding to go to university (where she excelled). She told her how painful it had been not to be able to discuss the feelings she had had for women and how she had to go to others for emotional support. She left her mother stunned, incredulous.

Emily was relieved, even liberated. Her father did not yet know, but that would come when the moment was right. Emily had an increased sense of self-esteem and self-confidence. This was heightened even further when, six months later, her mother informed her of a play she had seen about a gay man who was not accepted by his family after his disclosure. Her mother showed some signs of understanding, and even began to welcome Emily's female companion into her home with genuine warmth. Despite these signs of softening, Emily's mother continues to believe that Emily will eventually meet the "right" man, whom she will marry, and go on to lead a "normal" life.

Emily felt she could not tell her father directly, she asked her mother to do it. Her father's response: "I suspected it all along." She and her father have never spoken about her sexual orientation; however, she is certain that, for him, female homosexuality is of much less concern than male homosexuality.

Emily certainly experienced what many gays and lesbians experience—the plight of feeling alone. It was initially difficult for her to discuss her feelings with her family out of a fear of being rejected. As difficult as it was, and as hard as her mother received the news, Emily was extremely lucky. She was not exiled from the family; she was not rejected. And, with the passage of time, the initial hurt, especially on the part of her mother and sister, has gradually dissipated.

• a father's disbelief

When Marcel was ten years old, he had no difficulty recognizing his homosexuality. As far as he was concerned, he had been homosexual since birth, and so what? Young children can experience sexual arousal.

Down the street lived a fifteen-year-old boy to whom Marcel was sexually attracted. Marcel approached the boy and asked him if he would like to play with him in his treehouse. The boy accepted, and when both boys were inside, Marcel began to fondle the older boy. To Marcel's surprise, the boy accepted the fondling and began to reciprocate. Before they knew it, they were both naked. That's when Marcel's mother arrived. When his father came home that night, he flew into a rage and was ready to go to the fifteen-year-old's house and beat him into oblivion. Instead he gave Marcel a thrashing when he discovered that Marcel had initiated the whole episode.

For the next few years, Marcel's father's anger was ever-present, usually just below the surface, but sometimes front and center. He could not understand homosexuality; he loathed it, and his son could not be a homosexual person. He simply refused to consider that possibility. He took Marcel from psychiatrist to psychiatrist, looking for a "cure." Finally, Marcel had had enough. At age eighteen, he fled. His father would not have to have a "queer" son around the house.

Marcel is now an adult, working as a house painter. Though he has had multiple partners, he currently lives alone. He has never had a long-term relationship and readily admits he doesn't know how to have one. He never learned how to live in a compatible way with another human being as he never saw that type of relationship at home.

Fortunately for Marcel, he has always maintained a close relationship with his mother. His parents continue to live together, and he does see his father from time to time, but their relationship is cool. His father was never an affectionate man at the best of times; whatever affection he had shown Marcel in childhood has long since vanished. A pall hangs over the family.

• understanding prejudice

Too many families, unfortunately, are so blinded by homophobic beliefs that they cannot find the wherewithal to embrace a family member who professes his or her homosexual orientation.

Where do these beliefs and prejudices come from? First, they are *acquired,* learned; they are not instinctual or genetic. This is an important point since what we learn we can unlearn; we can alter our point of view, adopt a different perspective, particularly if we come to rely on credible information and not simply on unsubstantiated rumor, hearsay or bias.

Our prejudices stem from many sources, but surely the home must be the primary one. Our parents teach us by what they say, what they do, what they don't do, what they believe. Our personalities and value systems start to take shape in infancy under the influence and example of our parents; it's inescapable. But this influence is not irreversibly imprinted on our psyches and into our behavior patterns. As we become exposed to the outside world, to school, to community organizations, to books, to the media, to society in general, we begin to question our prejudices and beliefs, or they become reinforced, or we acquire new ones.

Prejudice has its comforts. If we are in the company of others who share our prejudices, we become less anxious. As the number of people who share our prejudices increases, any nagging doubts we may have about the correctness of our prejudices decreases.

But the prejudice may be dead wrong. Prejudice is very often built upon myths and misconceptions, upon half-truths or no truth. How can we know something is "true"? Truth is elusive, but the pursuit of it is within our power.

Parents of gay and lesbian children, especially parents who are encumbered by prejudices, can help free themselves by seeking information about homosexuality. This is not hard to do: there are books on the topic; there are resource centers, at least in larger cities; there is the Internet. There are support groups, such as PFLAG, and there are your gay and lesbian children and their friends, and the network of people and groups that they know about.

We do research about many aspects of our daily lives. We learn facts about the car we want to buy; we get different plans for the renovations we make in our homes; we explore the schools our children should attend; and on and on. How illuminating and helpful it would be, therefore, should we discover that one of our children is gay or lesbian, to find out something about homosexuality: the psychological and social aspects, the trials that are part of coming out, the barriers society places in the path of gays and lesbians.

• to tell or not to tell

Irwin grew up in an era of zero tolerance for any expression of same-sex preference. He would be the first one in his social circle to tell homophobic jokes; he would openly applaud newspaper reports of gay-bashing. He believed that gay men chose their lifestyle, and did so because they were weak, afraid of women, dominated by their mothers. Perhaps, he thought, they were cursed by Satan. He wasn't all that religious, but the Satan idea satisfied his sense of disgust for homosexual men. He had read somewhere that homosexuality was considered a mental aberration and that gays who really wanted to change could do so; they could exorcise the devil within them, so to speak.

In his youth, there was a lot less publicity about lesbianism. He had heard of it, but it wasn't the kind of thing that made the newspapers. The common prejudice was that all gay men were effeminate, and all effeminate men were gay. It was, therefore, relatively easy to know whether a man was gay or not. With women it was different; the difference between a lesbian or straight woman wasn't all that obvious, so there was less written or known about them. But, of course, whenever the subject of lesbians came up, Irwin's level of disgust was just as high as it was with homosexual men.

The first of Irwin's three children was a daughter, Pamela-Jane (P.J., for short). P.J. was a spirited, bright little girl, and the sole object of Irwin and Alicia's attention, until their son was born five years later. P.J. readily accepted little Danny, and then little Ronny, who was born about a year and a half later. There was great camaraderie—many family outings. It was a happy time.

In P.J.'s last year of high school, at age eighteen, she dropped the bombshell: she announced that she was a lesbian. Irwin was beside himself. His response was uncontrollable rage and disgust. Alicia, too, was stunned. She had had no idea, but she wasn't as hysterical as Irwin. Her response was in the order of: Maybe it's a mistake? Maybe there's something we can do? It was all Alicia could do to restrain Irwin from banishing P.J. from the house.

How could this happen to him? Irwin wondered. It wasn't possible.

Dannny and Ronny had grown up in a homophobic home, but they had also grown up in an era of some enlightenment and understanding of the gay world. They had gay school friends. They knew of girls who were lesbians. Their experience was different from their dad's. They tried to calm him down, pointing out that their sister had been a great friend to them and still was; that they didn't care what she was sexually. Irwin wasn't so irrational and so detached that these words didn't touch him. He calmed down a lot.

Nonetheless, he couldn't understand it. He turned over and over in his mind as many moments in P.J.'s upbringing as he could recall. He tried to fabricate stories and excuses, "reasons" for her homosexuality. But these constructions fell apart, and he was left with a huge chasm of ignorance and self-doubt. His family doctor had cared for the family for years. He would seek his counsel.

Dr. Ramjanathan was a wise and gentle man. He had seen Irwin and Alicia through many trying moments with Alicia's parents and with their children. Irwin trusted him. Dr. Ramjanathan suggested that Irwin learn more about homosexuality. There were books he could turn to, there was a gay and lesbian information center, there was a parents' support group.

I could never go to a group, Irwin thought. I would appear to be a failure if I commiserated with other parents. Besides, no one has to know, he thought. But he did go to the gay and lesbian information center. That turned the tide. The gay man who was in attendance that afternoon didn't "look or speak gay"—the first gay myth to be exploded. Furthermore, he was a civil and intelligent person who had patience for Irwin's agitation. Irwin got some written material and was directed to other sources.

It took Irwin two years to come to grips with his deeply entrenched prejudices. At the end of that time he had read thousands of pages about homosexuality, had attended many seminars, and had become an active member of the parents' support group. Alicia encouraged him and participated with him in a mutual quest for more knowledge and understanding. Irwin had gone through a period of remorse over his initial erratic behavior, but he was helped out of it, first and foremost, by P.J., and also by Alicia, the boys and Dr. Ramjanathan.

As bitter as his homophobia had been, Irwin was an intelligent man who loved his daughter, and was able to divert himself from a course of action that would have meant the end of family life as he'd come to know it, and the happiness of all concerned.

Irwin and his younger brother, Kent, had never been bosom buddies but they were able to communicate with each other reasonably well. About ten years after P.J. came out, their mother was admitted to the hospital with a terminal illness. Irwin and Kent were attending to her needs. They were the only children and both had a strong sense of family. Their mother had been the focal point that brought Irwin, Alicia and their three children together with Kent, his wife and two sons. They had been close to their parents, and her impending death weighed heavily upon them.

Kent wanted to meet Irwin for lunch. Irwin expected further discussion about mother. Instead, Kent wanted to talk about himself.

"Something is weighing so heavily on me, Irwin, and I don't know what to do."

"What is it, Kent?"

"Mother is about to die and there's a secret of major significance that I've kept from her all these years. I don't know if I should tell her. I don't know if I can."

"Can you tell me?"

Kent hesitated. Tears came to his eyes. "I'm gay."

Irwin sat in stunned silence.

"You've been through it, Irwin. You know what this means. I should have told you years ago. First of all, with all that homophobia that you displayed for so many years, I could hardly tell you that I was gay. Then, after what you experienced with P.J. and the change you went through—well, I knew you would be supportive, or I thought you would be, but I just didn't have the courage. P.J. was a single girl. I am a married man with two kids. I couldn't come out then. But now, with Mother on her deathbed, I'll feel guilty if I tell, and guilty if I don't. I don't know what to do."

Irwin regained his composure. He saw the suffering on his brother's face and knew he had to reach out to him. "Kent, you know that I support you, something I couldn't have said prior to the awakening I experienced after P.J. came out. I'm sorry I didn't make it easy for you to tell me. I'm not sure whether you should tell Mother or not, and I can't say yea or nay. But you know our mother. She is a tough woman who's heard a few tough things in her life. If you think that telling her will be her death blow—I don't think so. She's going to die from her cancer, not from you telling her you're gay.

"Who knows how she'll respond. I can tell you she was pretty upset with my behavior when I learned that P.J. was a lesbian. She wasn't happy about P.J. but she said I was still her father and she was still my daughter and I shouldn't reject her. I don't think she's going to reject you.

"Think about this. If you don't tell her, there's a good chance you'll always be wondering whether you should have told her or not. Think about it."

Kent did tell his mother. She didn't die on the spot. She did die soon after, though. Kent felt a great sense of relief that his lifelong lie had finally come to an end.

II

understanding why your child is gay

• chapter four

• common myths
and misconceptions

Harry and Joanne never, for a moment, suspected their son was gay. Joanne was quite articulate as she described the response she and Harry had after Tony came out:

"Our gay son, Tony, is the oldest of our four children. We had no suspicion in his youth. He excelled at individual sports. He was obviously a gifted artist. We're not sure when he really understood he was gay, because, at the age of twenty-three, he married a beautiful gal who he loved very much. But, two years later, he informed us that the marriage was breaking down, and he was honest enough to tell us the reason—he was gay. We needed a lot of education about homosexuality, but we were so preoccupied with his marriage breakdown that we weren't able to look for causes at that point. We were very superficial in our acceptance and tried to be as helpful as possible. Tony made an effort to give us as much information as he could, or as we were able to absorb. There wasn't all that much information available in those days. The main thing we heard about back then was how homosexual men were dying of AIDS. You can well imagine how much reassurance we needed. Tony was very good at calming us down."

The manner in which Joanne told her story was striking on several accounts. First, she did not speak with anger or resentment. She did not respond as if some terrible fate had befallen her and Harry. She was pragmatic. She was concerned that Tony should not suffer some sort of dire consequence of his homosexuality. She wanted to know the "cause." She wanted to know if all the rumors about homosexuality were true. She needed help in separating myth from fact.

"Once the dust around the marriage breakup settled, the full impact of Tony's homosexuality really hit us, and hit us hard. We didn't know any homosexuals, nor did we know any families who had a homosexual member, at least none that was out in the open. We're very pragmatic people. We have a simple philosophy of life: If there's a problem, find out the cause, then come up with the options for fixing it. Don't just whine about it, do something and get on with it.

"Right off the bat we got stuck. How was it possible that a son of ours could be homosexual, or "gay," as it's now called? How did that happen? Where did we go wrong? *Did* we go wrong? Is it genetic? But we didn't know of any other gay person in our family. Is it something that we did or didn't do, say or didn't say, when he was growing up? But we treated Tony's two brothers and one sister the same way, and they're not gay, as far as we know. Was it the fact that he was the eldest and we treated him with more anxiety than the others because, by the time they came along, we were more experienced parents?

"The two of us began to hear some scary things at that time. You know, if you're not involved in something, you might hear or know almost nothing about it. But once you're touched by an illness or a situation, it's amazing how you begin to hear things, and in those days most of the things we heard were scary, like how those friends of friends were getting a divorce because they fell apart after learning their son was gay.

"Well, we didn't fall apart, and our marriage wasn't threatened, but we were perplexed, very perplexed, about how it happened that our son was a homosexual. All he saw in our house was heterosexual love. We were strong churchgoers, still are. There was nothing feminine about the way we brought Tony up. He is a good artist. Could that have anything to do with it? But he was also a strong athlete. Did the soft side outweigh the masculine side? Did that sort of thinking even make any sense?"

Harry agonized: "Was I a poor role model? Did I not show him enough strength, enough leadership? Did my show of affection toward him influence his sexual orientation?"

Joanne kept going over details of how she dealt with Tony when he was growing up: "Was I too forceful a mother? Should I have stopped him from masquerading as a woman on Halloween when he was seven? Should I have encouraged his art? Maybe it happened when I was pregnant with him. I smoked back then. Once I fell on the ice."

Harry and Joanne continued to search for the "cause." The fact that they couldn't find one frustrated them. In the end, they saw that whether they knew the cause or not, they had to get on with living with the reality. The contentment on Tony's face helped them do that.

When you hear that your child is gay or lesbian, what really disturbs you about this newfound knowledge (if, indeed, you are disturbed at all)? Do you say (as the American Psychiatric Association did many years ago, but has since reversed its opinion) that homosexuality is an "illness" for which you must find a doctor to institute treatment? And, even if you believed this with heart and soul, whose best interests do you really have in mind—yours or your child's?

Self-deception is a powerful tool we humans use to assuage our feelings of anxiety, guilt, helplessness. We can deceive ourselves into believing all sorts of things: our problems are really someone else's fault; I did this, not because I really wanted to, but because he/she/they/the circumstances forced me to do it; I'm doing this for her own good, and so on. We sometimes blame others, deny responsibility or rationalize our motivation.

Most of us do not know much about homosexuality. In our search to either understand or condemn it, we may rely on well-known "facts" to be added to the storehouse of arguments we are gathering to make our case. By dispelling these myths, we can also dispel some of the prejudices we hold about gays and lesbians. Let's examine a few of those myths and misconceptions.

1. myth: all homosexual men are pedophiles

The adult son of friends of ours asked me to fill out a form reference letter on his behalf to accompany his application to become a Big Brother. Our young friend, Wynn, thought he would be providing a valuable public service, and have an enjoyable time, by being a friend and mentor to a boy who either had no father or had been deserted by his father. One of the questions on the form letter I was asked to complete dealt with the applicant's sexual preference: Was he homosexual? Where did this question come from? What business was it of anyone to ask such a question? Of what relevance was his sexual orientation to the performance of his function as a Big Brother? Could this organization that provided such a wonderful service to society, believe that a homosexual Big Brother is more likely than a heterosexual Big Brother to sexually assault or corrupt the boys under his charge? Where did this stereotype of the gay male come from?

Pedophiles—primarily, but not exclusively, males—are sexually attracted to young children, and occasionally to infants, of either sex. There are multiple ways in which the pedophile will act on his sexual inclination. Often he will seduce his victims, who may comply out of ignorance or fear, or even a desire to participate. The child may also resist or run away. The scenarios vary, but some of them end in tragedy.

Unfortunately, pedophilic practices are widespread. Thousands of pedophiles are apprehended each year, and probably many thousands more go unrecognized because their activites are never reported. Even when children do inform their parents, that information is often disbelieved or passed over, especially if the perpetrator is a close family friend or a relative.

No characteristic features mark the pedophile. He is very often a heterosexual, with a wife and children of his own. In his adult life, he seeks sexual gratification with an adult female. In his subterranean life, he seeks a sexual liaison with a prepubertal boy or girl. Pedophiles are found in every stratum of society. The man's adult sexual preference, whether heterosexual or homosexual, does not dictate his pedophilic propensity. Homosexual men have unfairly been branded as having an inbred pedophilic tendency. The majority of homosexual men are no more likely to have this tendency than are the majority of heterosexual men.

Society and many of its institutions, particularly those dealing with children, have this irrational idea that gay men are after the children of the world, especially boys. This misperception has given us a communal fear of entrusting our children to homosexual men. The majority of men who are sexually attracted to young boys have absolutely no interest in having sex with an adult male. There is no link between adult male homosexuality and pedophilia.

Consider your own gay son. You have come to terms with the fact of his homosexuality, or you are struggling to understand it, or you're still in a state of total rejection. In whatever stage you find yourself, can you honestly say that, because your son is gay, he is also a pedophile, that he is sexually attracted to children, that he is danger to them?

2. myth: homosexual males are likely to develop AIDS

Acquired immune deficiency syndrome (AIDS) is a major public-health concern because of the high mortality rate associated with the syndrome, because of the lack of a cure and because of its dramatic increase around the world. It's a disease all parents worry about, because it can be sexually transmitted. When AIDS first came to public attention in North America, that attention focused on the fact that the majority of victims seemed to be gay men. Male homosexuality was, therefore, considered to be a risk factor for the development of AIDS. Although that risk continues to exist, it does not automatically follow that all gay men have AIDS or are destined to get it. AIDS knows no boundaries. There is now predominantly heterosexual infectivity. Men, women and children are being infected on a global scale.

AIDS is caused by the human immunodeficiency virus (HIV). Not everyone infected with the virus has a symptomatic case of AIDS, but, whether symptomatic or not, a person who carries the virus can infect another person. That person, in turn, can either become quickly symptomatic or can develop symptoms of AIDS at a later date. An "AIDS test" is actually a blood test, not for the AIDS virus (HIV), but for an antibody to HIV. Antibodies are chemical compounds formed by the body's defense system to try to combat substances that enter the body but are not native to it. HIV antibodies don't form immediately, but may take up to six months to develop. The presence of antibodies doesn't mean that the person already has AIDS, but it does mean that there is the probability of developing AIDS at some time in the future because the virus is now present in the body.

When one first becomes infected with HIV, there may be very little indication of it. In about 70 percent of cases, there is a flu-like illness, with or without swelling of the lymph nodes. There may also be ulcers in infected areas. There may then follow an asymptomatic period, during which the individual is perfectly well. Does AIDS inevitably develop if one is infected with HIV? The true answer is probably unknown, but there are people who were infected ten or more years previously but are yet to manifest the characteristic illnesses associated with AIDS.

As the name implies, AIDS is a syndrome in which the immune system has broken down and is no longer functioning at its full capacity. Infections to which the body is ordinarily immune can now invade, causing symptoms such as weakness, fatigue, nausea, vomiting, weight loss, diarrhea and breathlessness. There are drugs to help ward off the infections and deal with symptoms, but unfortunately there is not yet a cure for AIDS.

How does one acquire the virus? There are two major ways: sexual contact and sharing drug injection needles. In addition, the virus may be passed from an infected mother to her child before birth or during delivery. The virus may also be found in breast milk.

What concerns us here the most is the sexual transmission of the virus. The virus can be found in various bodily fluids, including blood, semen, and secretions from ulcers and open sores. When an open wound or abrasion where blood vessels have been damaged is exposed to the virus, HIV can gain entry into the body. The virus is particularly drawn to the various constituents of semen: not only fluid, but sperm and other types of cells. The seminal fluid and the cells may contain high levels of the virus even when blood levels have been reduced by anti-HIV treatment. An HIV-infected man or woman, therefore, can spread the virus to a sexual partner if the partner already has an abrasion, or if an abrasion occurs during contact, through which the AIDS virus can then pass.

Sexual transmission of HIV can be significantly curtailed by use of a condom. Unfortunately, despite knowing what safe sex means and what its advantages are, many individuals throw caution to the wind, believing "It can't happen to me." Homosexual men are not the exclusive recipients of this virus. There is a significant increase, worldwide, in the acquisition of HIV through heterosexual contact. In 1995, it was estimated that, of all those in the world with HIV, 40 percent were women. An American study, published in the *New England Journal of Medicine* in 1998, found that, of an estimated 231,400 HIV-infected individuals, 23 percent were women. In this same study, the percentage of individuals in each risk category was as follows: injection-drug use (24 percent), men having sex with men (49 percent), heterosexual contact (18 percent), other (9 percent). Women are not immune from contracting HIV from sexual contact with each other, nor from the subsequent development of AIDS. It is the sexual practice that is the risk factor, not the identity. Women are much more likely to contract AIDS from sex with a man than from sex with a woman.

What does all of this mean in practical terms for your family? Everyone—homosexual, heterosexual, men, women, children—is susceptible to contracting the AIDS virus. While scientists are trying to find a cure for the disease, it is up to the rest of us to do our utmost to prevent its spread. Prevention means barring access of the virus to our blood-circulation system, that is, through injection into our veins or through sores or lesions or ulcers into which the virus can enter. The primary vehicle for "safe sex" is the condom.

If the largest number of AIDS infections in North America occurs in males who have engaged in homosexual practices, it is not that AIDS is the exclusive property of homosexual men;

rather, it is that no appropriate preventative measures were taken. All of society must be vigilant.

3. myth: gays and lesbians are more prone to get hepatitis than are heterosexuals

Hepatitis, or inflammation of the liver, is an extremely common source of ill health. It is most often caused by one of several types of viruses that, from an acute stage, may progress to severe liver destruction (cirrhosis) and even to liver cancer. The two major viruses that can cause hepatitis are the hepatitis B virus (HBV) and hepatitis C virus (HCV).

Both viruses can be transmitted sexually, but HBV is much more likely than HCV to be transmitted in this way. The overwhelming majority of HCV carriers have acquired the virus from shared needles for intravenous drug use or through shared straws for snorting cocaine. Obviously one's sexual orientation has no bearing on this mode of transmission; heterosexual and homosexual individuals are equally susceptible to acquiring hepatitis C. Controversy surrounds the ease with which HCV can be transmitted sexually. It appears that the likelihood of spreading hepatitis C increases with multiple sexual exposures; that is, the chances of contracting hepatitis C escalate with the number of sexual partners. Hepatitis C may also be contracted through blood transfusions but today this risk is very low because of careful screening of donors' blood.

A fact about hepatitis B that is not common knowledge is that it is about 100 times more infectious than AIDS. But, like AIDS, hepatitis is a preventable disease if the appropriate precautions are taken.

HBV can be found in bodily fluids of infected people, fluids to which other people may be exposed through sexual contact, through sharing needles, or through occupational hazards. The prevalence of HBV varies globally. In South-East Asia, China and Africa, more than 50 percent of the population may become infected with HBV at some time in their lives, and about 8 percent remain chronic carriers of the virus. In the Western world and Australia the endemic level of infection is much lower. In one study of 228 gay men with no obvious risk factors except sexual activity, 34.4 percent were found to have been infected with HBV. There appeared to be a relationship between infectivity and various types of unprotected anal sexual activity. Gay men infected with HCV (3–12 percent) acquired this infection primarily through drug injections rather than sexual activity.

Today, parents in general are concerned about the possibility of their children acquiring infections through sexual contact or by any other route. All parents should be aware of the health risks of unprotected sex, in particular, and consider the following:

• Seek out information on all sexually transmitted diseases, especially AIDS and hepatitis.
• Pass this information along to your son or daughter.
• Suggest that your child see a doctor for testing, even if only to know that baseline tests are normal. The results of such testing can be used for comparison purposes with later tests.
• Suggest that your child's partners also be informed about sexually transmitted diseases.

4. myth: all gay men are transvestites

In our society few of us would turn our heads upon seeing a woman wearing some form of male clothing. A prime example is a woman wearing slacks or jeans. It seems even naive to use this as an example since the wearing of slacks by women is part of the general community's custom. Even less common articles of men's apparel—for example, ties, shirts, blazers, oxfords— are unlikely to turn heads. But a man in women's clothes is likely to be noticed.

Women's clothing on men is simply not part of our cultural tradition. When we see a man dressed this way, does the label "homosexual" spring to mind? Men do wear women's clothing in a variety of circumstances. Those circumstances, however, do not define those men as homosexual. Some of them may be, of course, since gay men make up a significant proportion of all societies.

The practice among men of wearing women's clothing is known as transvestism or cross-dressing. This phenomenon is not rare, but how common it is no one really knows since most men who engage in this practice do so either in private or discreetly (i.e., they wear women's underclothing). One thing we do know is that the majority of men who cross-dress are heterosexual.

Transvestites, for the most part, are men who are erotically stimulated by the wearing of female clothes. They will often fantasize a heterosexual experience while cross-dressed or while caressing an article of female clothing, bringing themselves to orgasm by masturbation. Cross-dressing is practised by all cultural or social traditions and groups.

There is one example of transvestitism which is not transvestitism in the true sense of the word, and that is the "cross-dressing" of the transsexual. A transsexual or transgender individual, who can be either male or female, believes that his or her true gender is the opposite of the external body. A male transsexual strives to have a female body, and "cross-dressing" in this instance is a logical extension of his (her) "true" gender. The same is true for a female transsexual who strives to have a male body.

5. myth: gays are effeminate; lesbians are masculine

Of all the stereotypical ideas about gay men and lesbian women, this one is dominant. There certainly are gay men who have feminine behavioral features, and lesbian women who have masculine ones. But there are also heterosexual men and women whose behavioral patterns could be ascribed to those of the opposite sex. Mannerisms are not an indicator of sexuality: By far, the overwhelming majority of homosexual men and women exhibit no outward manifestation of their erotic orientation. If we relied on this stereotypic description of gays and lesbians to ascertain sexual orientation we would generally be wrong.

Gay men and women do not strive to become the opposite sex. That quest belongs to the transsexual. Gay men and women are clear about their gender—in body and mind. This question of "femininity" in gay men, however, is one that has received some attention in research literature because of the widely held belief that gay men are somewhere between being truly "male" and truly "female." Gay women and the proclivity for "masculinity" is a subject that has not been studied nearly to the same extent. Studies going back to the 1930s and 1940s suggested that it would be possible to distinguish masculinity from femininity on the basis of attitudes, behaviors and preferences. In the twenty-first century we recognize that the differences between male and female attitudes and behaviors have become quite blurred.

The old research scales of masculinity and femininity based on gender role (behavior) have, to a large extent, been replaced by assessments of gender identity, that is, the self-perceptions of males and females, rather than their "behaving" as males or females would be "expected" to behave. (Today it is not uncommon, for example, for a father to take paternity leave from his job to look after a newborn baby while the child's mother returns to work. This behavior would previously have been considered female.)

A gender-identity scale was originally developed in the 1970s by Dr. Kurt Freund, a psychiatrist at the University of Toronto. The scale was later modified to remove questions with a behavioral bias (that is, those that promoted a stereotypical view of the roles men and women were expected to play as opposed to those that elicited the subject's view of himself as masculine or feminine). A study of homosexual and heterosexual men conducted by Drs. Sanders (a psychiatrist), Langevin (a psychologist), and me found that, in total, the homosexual group had a higher feminine gender-identity score; this finding was interpreted as showing less "masculinity" in self-perception, and more "femininity," but the perception was deemed masculine nonetheless. Moreover, only about 57 percent of those in the homosexual group showed this tendency toward reduced "masculinity." This tendency toward a higher female gender identity (decreased "masculinity") is not, however, confined strictly to a subset of homosexual men. Highly educated heterosexual men also demonstrate this trend according to various personality scales. This finding may reflect a flaw in the way these rating scales are conceived and developed rather than a significant diversion from what is a fundamental male self-perception.

In our study, it was also shown that heterosexual men preferred female partners who, in general, were "feminine," that is, lighter, shorter, physically weaker, and with typically female rounded hips. Homosexual men, whether of increased or low feminine gender identity, had no such clear preferences in the physical attributes of their male partners.

There is no established cause- and-effect relationship between effeminate behavior and male homosexuality. Nor is there any between masculine behavior and lesbianism. Mannerisms that are considered to be those of the opposite sex may be acquired, not because of a natural consequence of the underlying homosexual erotic preference, but because, in a world that is so strongly heterosexual, these may be a way of attracting the attention of potential same-sex partners. Opposite-sex mannerisms are more common among gay men than are male mannerisms in gay women possibly because lesbians are more fluid in their sexual experiences, which can include male partners, especially near the outset of their sexual interaction with others.

6. myth: sexual orientation can be changed

For the most part, when you have something that requires fixing, you are usually less interested in why the thing got broken in the first place than in how it can be repaired. Take your car, for example. You hear a rattle or feel a jerkiness. Most of us aren't interested in the mechanics of the problem; we simply take the car to a service station and hope that the service person will diagnose the problem and fix it. We want to drive away from that service station in the car we used to know and trust.

But when you discover that a loved one is homosexual and you are surprised, disappointed, shocked, stunned, speechless, angered, hostile, does adopting the "squeaky car" attitude help you? Do you want to rush your loved one off to the medical or psychological service station and have him or her fixed and returned to you with no further homoerotic tendencies?

Discovering that your child is lesbian or gay is not the same as discovering that your car is broken. Most likely, the person who needs to be repaired, or made whole, is not the lesbian or gay child but you.

One way to achieve that wholeness is to have some knowledge, some understanding, not simply about homosexuality, but about sexuality in general.

• *sex and gender*

Let's start at the beginning, at conception. That is the starting point of your sexuality because, at conception, when a sperm fertilizes an egg, we are given genetic material from both the egg and the sperm. One of the things this genetic material will do (or is intended to do) is determine whether you will be male or female. The genetic determination of your sex lies within the sex chromosomes you inherit from your mother and father.

Chromosomes are strands of chemical substances, nucleic acids, that are joined together. Along the whole length of each chromosome are groups of these nucleic acids, which constitute your genes. These direct a great number of encoded bodily actions and events that can occur only under the influence of genetic instruction. Your mother contributes twenty-three chromosomes and your father contributes twenty-three chromosomes to the fetus; thus, forty-six are found in each cell of the body. Each chromosome has its own unique genetic elements (pairings of the chemical constituents from the chromosome of the mother and the father). These pairings direct physical and chemical activities within the body; they determine the maximum height to which you will grow; they determine the color of your eyes and hair. Do they influence your behavior? Though scientists have looked for genetic markers when analyzing a variety of behaviors, including sexual ones, they have found no clear predetermining genetic factors.

The important point is that nobody knows why some people are homosexual and some people are heterosexual.

Even if the genetic program starts us in the direction of becoming either male or female, roadblocks or twists in the road may thwart nature's intention so that, at birth, a female may emerge with certain reproductive difficulties or a male may emerge who brings into this world one or more variations on the norm that may or may not be problematic in later life. Many men have such variations and don't even realize it. These include minor abnormalities in genital development, sperm production problems, excess breast development. What, then, can we say constitutes true masculinity?

The answer to this question covers not only physical development, but also gender identity, social upbringing and expectations of "others" (society, community, religion, etc.). At the end of the day, can we possibly come up with a simple, unified definition of masculinity? No.

Let me give you an example of a common type of glitch that occurs in the usual course of developing a male after conception. Males normally have forty-six chromosomes, two of them the sex chromosomes, x and y. What happens if somehow the mother contributed two x chromosomes, or the mother contributed one x chromosome and the father contributed both an x and a y. The result would be a male (because of the presence of a y chromosome) who would have forty-seven chromosomes; the extra chromosome designation would then be 47xxy instead of the usual designation for a male, 46xy. This set of circumstances is known as Klinefelter's syndrome, after the doctor who, with colleagues, first described this unusual chromosomal state in the 1940s.

Klinefelter's syndrome is not rare, occurring in about 1 in 400 or 500 live male births. A wide variety of symptoms may be present in those with Klinefelter's syndrome, but in the overwhelming majority of cases, no immediately apparent problem exists until either one of two situations presents itself. The primary bodily abnormality that Klinefelter's syndrome produces is defective testicular action in both of the two functions of the testes, testosterone secretion and sperm production. The sperm-producing portion of the testes (the seminiferous tubules) never forms normally in the first place; the testosterone-producing cells usually do work for several decades but are weak to begin with and eventually fail in keeping up with the body's need for testosterone.

Because of these two significant abnormalities in testicular function, most individuals with Klinefelter's syndrome present to their doctor with either infertility (the majority of patients are unable to produce any sperm whatsoever) or symptoms of low blood-testosterone levels (erectile difficulty, decreased energy). There is no treatment for the absent sperm production; there is treatment for the decreased testosterone production–namely, lifelong administration of testosterone. Despite these two testicular abnormalities, nobody disputes the fact that individuals with Klinefelter's syndrome are clearly and distinctly male.

Just as we cannot change our genetic makeup, the number and nature of our chromosomes and genes (although genetic engineering is working on that), we cannot change our sexual orientation. If you learn that your child is gay or lesbian and you have ideas about changing that orientation, forget it. Don't rush off to the psychiatrist expecting the doctor to reset the switch from homosexuality to heterosexuality; it can't be done. It is possible that you or your child may need the help of a psychiatrist or psychologist, not to change orientation, but to enable one or both of you to deal with the anxiety that accompanies that unchangeable fact of life.

• *what is masculine?*
Society has stereotypical views of what it considers masculinity to be. We see this stereotype expressed in books, magazines, television programs, television commercials and movies: a young, handsome, strong man, presumably heterosexual as demonstrated by the number of beautiful women who usually surround him. His big muscles allow him to do the most arduous of tasks, whether in the gym, on the job, at home or in strenuous recreational or sporting activity.

There are many things, however, that we do not know about this idyllic man. How well does he get on with his fellow human beings? What prejudices does he have about other people or groups of people? Is he tender-hearted? Is he capable of crying at emotionally heart-wrenching scenes in the movies? Is he a kind, considerate person? What's more important to him—his looks or the nature of his humanity and his ability to be sensitive to others? Would he be willing to wash the dishes, take out the garbage and vacuum the carpets? Is he a person who can easily be helpful to others without expecting some sort of reward or recognition for that helpfulness? Is he a self-sufficient man, with true self-confidence? Can he be his own person without succumbing to peer pressure to drink, smoke, do drugs or engage in any activity that truly doesn't interest him?

There are a few other things we don't know about our "ideal" masculine man. We don't know the size of his testicles. We don't know about his sexual orientation. We don't know about his chromosomal and genetic makeup. We don't know about his fertility capacity. We don't know whether he is a genetic female (chromosome profile 46xx) who has had a sex-change operation and is now a male.

There are two concepts that need clarification: maleness and masculinity. *Maleness* is biologically based, *masculinity* is behaviorally based. From the biological perspective, the idea of *maleness* is fairly straightforward. A male is a person whose genetic makeup includes at least one y chromosome, who looks like a male, who has testes and a penis, who produces testosterone to which his body is capable of responding (there are some women who produce as much testosterone as a man but are not capable of responding to it). Men are expected to produce sperm (but this does not invariably happen, as we noted in discussing Kline-felter's syndrome or other states of abnormal testicular function). So a man is unquestionably a male even if he has problems with testosterone and sperm production.

It's more difficult to offer a definition of the concept of *masculinity* that everybody can agree upon, since masculinity is really a behavioral idea and not a biological one. Once we start trying to define a concept based on behavioral features, we can run into serious disagreements based on personal prejudices and biases; for example, is physical strength a necessary prerequisite for masculinity? If we say yes, then we are led down the rocky road of disillusionment. Let us say a man becomes weak, either from extreme exertion or because of illness. Does such a man cease being masculine? Or let us say that a man has an attribute that is usually thought of as feminine (whatever such an attribute might be). Does this man then lose his masculinity?

Now let us consider the man whose sexual partner is another man. Has some authority somewhere defined the masculine man as being heterosexual? Hardly. The idea of masculinity seems to have very little relevance in reality.

• *what is feminine?*

Despite women's liberation, despite the fact that women have careers, despite the fact that women do things that were traditionally done by men, society still has a stereotypical view of women. The general view of women has clearly undergone some changes since Betty Friedan wrote her important book, *The Feminine Mystique*, in 1963. However, despite her efforts to raise public awareness, there still persists today a stereotypical view of what it means to be feminine. If you do not fit the rigid definition of femininity, then you are thought of as something other than the ideal female. Young girls starve themselves to be thin. Older women often resort to endless diets and plastic surgery to attain the ideal "feminine" mold.

There was a time when everyone seemed to have a clear vision of what it meant to be feminine. Girls, and subsequently women, were sweet; they looked nice, they smelled nice, they did nice things. Women had long hair, wore dresses and cried easily because of their emotional nature. Women were soft and did soft things. They were best suited to raising children and keeping house.

This distorted vision included a particular view of female sexuality—that all women (and all men, for that matter) were heterosexual. Not only was woman heterosexual, but it was her responsibility to ensure that her husband's sexual needs were well looked after. It was assumed either that she had no sexual needs, or that, if she did, they were of secondary importance, superseded by those of her husband. It was never considered that women had sexual needs to which their husbands might pay particular attention. And, of course, women's sexuality was always thought of in relation to a husband since sex outside of marriage was forbidden to women.

These stereotypical ideas seem depressingly naive at the beginning of the twenty-first century. Nonetheless, in many parts of the world women are still subject to these archaic views. The more we resist changing our views, the more we refuse to recognize that human behavior has wide possibilities, the longer it will take us to understand and accept the normalcy of multiple variations in human behavior, including sexual practices.

Today, women wear hard hats, drive buses, become police

officers and chief executive officers, play hockey, commit crimes, go to jail. Women sometimes don't cry when we expect them to. Women love men. Women love women.

• overcoming myths and misconceptions

A psychiatrist I know grew up with traditional values and stereotypical ideas about men and women—their psyches, their emotions and their roles. He believes there is a feminine nature and that we should recognize it and accept it. He believes there are female emotions and male emotions, and that they are fixed and unchangeable. Many people believe this, but when a psychiatrist promotes the idea, it carries a certain weight, a certain credibility.

This thinking may originate in outmoded psychological theories that emerged not from scientific investigation and inquiry, but from the prejudices of a male-dominated society. The folklore and the sacred writings of most cultures throughout history promoted certain ideas of masculinity and femininity, and of sexual behavior. Cultures, not science or nature, established the rules believed to govern male and female behavior. To defy these rules was to defy the reason and logic of the time, and sometimes the various divine authorities that these cultures created and held up as immutable.

There is little evidence, however, to suggest an inborn nature in human beings. If we accept the theory that nature governs our behavior, we deny the existence of free will, and hence absolve ourselves of responsibility for our behaviour. We are, therefore, not the free individuals we believe ourselves to be and our actions must happen the way they happen.

But we are free; we can change. History has demonstrated that our concepts of male and female behavior and identity have changed. In modern times, gender roles change and interchange. To be masculine or feminine is not to fit into a precast mold. It is to be a unique creation, a unique human being. As we grow from childhood to adulthood, we bring with us a sexual orientation whose source has eluded us. It tracks with us from childhood, perhaps from infancy. But that orientation, too, does not predetermine the nature of our masculinity or femininity. Those traits are created out of the sum of our life's experiences.

One day, the idea of femininity and masculinity will fall by the wayside. We're a long way from that day, but it's an ideal toward which to strive. One day, we'll all be viewed simply as individual human beings with our own personal characteristics and traits that will serve as the basis upon which others will accept us, reject us, or simply tolerate us. This freedom to be ourselves is far preferable to the oppressive social demand that we be viewed as a particular kind of human being who fits this or that currently accepted model of behavior or set of characteristics. These models are always changing as society pits one against another. But we have a long way to go to free ourselves from the past.

Myths and misconceptions occupy every nook and cranny of our lives. They have great power in giving us comfort; they also create and bolster prejudices and, as a result, can be destructive—to others, to society and even to ourselves.

There is one simple, but fundamental truth about gays and lesbians: they are gay or lesbian because they are sexually attracted to individuals of their own sex. Beyond this truth lie only generalizations and misconceptions that can lead us into beliefs and behaviors that debase the human spirit.

• *chapter five*

• whose life is it?

A man and a woman marry. They have plans, they have visions
of how life will unfold for them. They deliberate about their
own personal careers, about where to live, about what furniture
to buy. They engage in activities individually, and together as a
couple. They may decide to have children.

When children arrive, parents nurture—with material
goods, with food and sustenance, with a place to live, with love
and caring and sympathy. Parents provide safety and security.
They provide a moral groundwork, passing on their beliefs,
opinions and values to their children. They try to instill in their
children an outlook on life, a mode of living, that is based on
their experience. Parents want their children to behave in a
particular manner for a number of reasons: (1) they believe it
will be good for the child, (2) they believe it is the right,
"normal" way to behave, (3) they think that "proper" behavior
in their children reflects well on the parents, (4) they believe
that children "should" obey their parents.

The meaning of life for many parents is their children. The
growth and development of children provide immense joy and

satisfaction. For many parents, the most significant of life's rewards is seeing their children flourish. For many parents, this is the only reward they allow themselves to have; they give meaning to their own lives through the lives of their children. Unfortunately, this is often carried to the extreme where parents expect their children to adopt the views, desires and culture that the parents themselves have come to live by. In such cases, parents are ill-prepared when their children do the unexpected.

The key to their unpreparedness is their expectation. Human expectations can often be clear and rational. We expect a sunny day if the meteorologists predict one. We expect Bob to meet us at 2:00 p.m. if we know from past experience that Bob is punctual. These are rational expectations based on previous knowledge or experience.

But into many areas of our life we introduce irrational or less reasonable expectations. We expect the boss to applaud us for our good work, but that applause never comes; we expect our spouses to respond in ways we think appropriate, then become angry, frustrated or upset when they don't behave as we would have. Having high expectations of others exposes us to the potential for anxiety. Having low expectations of others is more likely to leave us calm and serene.

Many parents expect their children to live life in a particular way—usually a clearly delineated heterosexual way. This means getting an education in preparation for gainful employment; finding a mate with whom to create a meaningful life; having children, thus providing the parents with grandchildren; and living in a manner that reflects well on the parents.

In many cultures in the world, parents' expectations are reinforced because community or social mores supersede individual wants, desires and freedoms. In these cultures, the community is primary, the individual is secondary. But in many other cultures in the world, particularly Western cultures, freedom is promoted as the primary value that takes precedence over family and social customs, as long it includes respect for persons and their property.

Individual liberty and freedom, therefore, are often at odds with society's expectations in general, and with those of parents in particular. Parents who expect society to respect their right to personal liberty should not be surprised that their own children expect the same right. This is as true of the traditional freedoms of assembly, the press and the vote, as it is of sexual orientation and the gender of one's love partner.

• Vickie's struggle

One of my female patients, Vickie, age twenty, an anorexic, came for a consultation, not because of her eating disorder, but because she had stopped having her periods. Her mother, an attractive, slim, forty-five year-old, accompanied her to the office. She tried to answer every question I asked Vickie, who was, of course, old enough not only to be there alone, but to have her right to medical confidentiality respected.

Vickie was a dancer. She had started dance lessons around the age of five. Her mother, Stephanie, had insisted that she study dance because she herself had been a dancer though her professional career ended the moment she became pregnant with Vickie. Stephanie's marriage to Vickie's father ended when Vickie was about eight. Stephanie wanted Vickie to become the great dancer that she felt she might have been had the pregnancy not intervened. Vickie's father thought that an eight-year-old child should be involved in other activities for eight-year-olds besides dancing. When it had become clear that dance had taken over, Vickie's father left.

Vickie's periods began around age fifteen. They were never regular, and they stopped completely when she was seventeen or eighteen. The diagnosis seemed obvious: Vickie ate very little but she perceived herself as fat and overweight and was encouraged in this obsession by Stephanie, who argued that dancers must always be slim and fit.

Vickie underwent the appropriate tests, and the hormonal investigation pointed to a suppression of the function of the pituitary gland (the master gland of the body). This suppression could be caused by a pituitary gland tumour, but X-ray studies ruled that out. The final diagnosis was anorexia nervosa, which Stephanie refused to consider or acknowledge. There must be something else wrong.

Despite their stubborn insistence that there was nothing unusual about Vickie's diet, eventually both Vickie and her mother started to understand that they must consider the diagnosis of anorexia, since Vickie was losing more weight and was now even less than the 98 pounds she weighed when she first came to me. Vickie was the one who finally agreed to undergo psychiatric treatment for what she now acknowledged was an eating disorder. She was then able to bring Stephanie around to the same realization.

After several months of psychiatric therapy, in which Stephanie participated from time to time, Vickie started to gain weight. At five feet, five inches in height, she had an ideal weight of about 120 pounds. When she reached 110 pounds, she had her first spontaneous period in years. Fortunately, she continued on the road to recovery. Her weight leveled off at about 117 pounds, and her periods became regular. She continued to dance, but less obsessively, and she began to include other things in her life. Stephanie entered psychiatric therapy for a profound depression.

This story underlines the cost of extremes in parental expectations. When Stephanie's dream of being a great dancer ended, she chose to live out her fantasy through her daughter, Vickie, who would be her surrogate in pursuing with passion the dream that Stephanie could never realize. Stephanie *expected* Vickie to live out this dream. But when Vickie became anorexic, even though this was in accord with her mother's view of a slim nubile dancer, she was rebelling subconsciously against being used by her mother.

We can expect things of our children, but we can't expect them to be us. This is as true of their sexual orientation as it is of anything else. We might expect our child to have a heterosexual orientation, but we cannot be certain that this will be the case. And, if it is not, then it need not be seen as a tragedy.

• the real you

On a day that you're alone at home, take all your clothes off and stand in front of a full-length mirror. Don't do this as part of getting dressed or undressed as a prelude to some other activity; do this as part of an act in itself. Just stand there. Observe yourself. No need to get edgy. No one else is there. You're alone.

The first thing you notice is just that: you're alone. There is no one there with whom you can connect, no one there to give you instruction or criticism or praise, no one there to make decisions for you, no one there to provide protection or to create obstacles or restrictions. You are it—at least for this moment, you are the only person in the world, and you are totally responsible for this, your world and for the decisions you make. There is a revolutionary idea here—one that is profound in its simplicity: you are free; you are not part of another; you are not part of a people or a nation or a group of any kind. You are alone and you are free. And freedom is something from which you cannot escape.

Now look at your body. It is unique. It is yours and no one else's. There are parts you do not like, there are parts you deem acceptable, there are parts that are superlative. This is the pure, unadulterated you. In your freedom, you can tousle your hair; you can stick out your tongue; you can wiggle your ears; you can flap your arms; you can touch your genitals and think any thought you wish. To be human is to be a sexual being, whether we express it in a flamboyant manner or repress it deeply in a subconscious abyss. It is there, somewhere. Our sexuality is composed, in part, of that naked body you see before you in the mirror. It is composed, in part, of what the mirror does not reflect—namely, all that we call soul, spirit, thought and the will to act.

Let's focus in on the mind for a moment. To be human is to be in charge of one's mind. The world can be viewed from many different perspectives, and from our own inner launching pad we can set out on a voyage of exploration to places we never imagined we could go, or that even existed.

At this moment of naked aloneness, we control our thoughts and our actions. Can we maintain that sense of personal power and freedom when we are in the presence of other human beings with whom we interact? Or do we succumb to the force of the "they," to all those stubborn influences that impose themselves on us at all times? Can we maintain the integrity of the solitary naked body standing in front of the mirror and a free and independent mind? Or do we allow the world around us to take over what is rightfully ours?

In the real world in everyday life, we do not stand naked before others. We hide our bodies; we hide our mind, cloaking it in the expectations of others. In doing so, we relinquish our freedom in order not to offend, in order to please, in order to win favor. We give up the real "we" in order to look, think and act like the Other. We hide the essential nakedness of our being because it might offend or upset or alienate others. That fear of alienation forces us to alienate ourselves.

• Jan's confusion

Jan recalls the intense struggle she endured in coming to terms with who she really was. It took her years of pain, promiscuity, and, finally, therapy, to recognize the person inside.

Jan had her first sexual encounter at age fifteen. He was the dream of the school, a terrific dancer, the star center of the basketball team, the idol of all the girls at the school. Jan was full of spunk, a real livewire. Our hero decided he was going to conquer her, although it was probably the other way around. In retrospect, Jan realized that she wasn't really physically attracted to him in an erotic fashion, but it was a challenge for her to have the school hero, or "Lover-Boy" as she later called him (LB for short), select her for a sexual outing. He fell perfectly into her master plan to seduce him.

It was at school, behind the locked door of the sports equipment room. With balls, bats, shoulder pads and other paraphernalia as their only witnesses, Jan and LB went at it, fondling each other while shedding their clothes. LB had a condom ready (Jan had one in reserve just in case) and, although he rarely fumbled on the basketball court, he was an absolute klutz in trying to open the condom container. Once he managed to put it on, the intensity of his ardor got the better of him and he ejaculated.

Although fast ejaculations are commonplace, especially among teenage boys, this was Jan's first real sexual encounter with a boy and she was mortified. To her, in her inexperience, the golden-boy hero was tarnished. Jan's initiation into the world of consensual sex was nothing short of a disaster.

She wondered what her girlfriends and the erotic books she read were talking about when they described the ecstasy of the sexual act. She thought to herself: "Maybe there *is* something to it. I'm not giving up so fast." Over the next two or three years, Jan conducted a series of "experiments," having a variety of sexual experiences with as many male partners as she could find. But only when she masturbated during one of these encounters did she achieve an orgasm. She began to believe that her first unsatisfying experience with LB had set the course for her particular pattern of sexual responsiveness and she was doomed to sexual misery.

This feeling of gloom and doom was intensified by the strange stirrings she began to experience around the time of the "Lover-Boy Disaster." She started to feel a surge of sexual electricity whenever she was with another girl or older woman in certain situations or positions. A female classmate bending over to pick up a dropped pencil and showing the outline of her buttocks and thighs, a woman brushing her hair and showing the contour of her breasts, the scent of a particular perfume wafting through the air—all had startling effect on Jan. There were times when she even experienced a spontaneous orgasm.

Jan, who had lived a rather sheltered, even conservative, life, had no idea what these sexual feelings meant. She felt that they were abnormal, and so turned to more encounters with men. The disgust she had experienced with LB colored each encounter, and she never reached the state of sexual arousal she attained through a simple glance at a woman. By the time Jan was eighteen, she was in an enormous state of confusion about her "abnormality." Why did she have such a pronounced sexual response to either seeing or imagining women, and why was she incapable of having similar responses when engaging in overt sexual activity with men?

Her grades in school suffered; her social life dwindled as she became more reclusive and ended her encounters with men; her anxiety level rose, and her self-confidence was almost totally shattered.

Then something happened that would change the course of her life. Something, which at the time seemed even more repulsive to her than the "Lover-Boy" charade, but which in retrospect was the seminal event which put her on the road to understanding herself and to dealing with that understanding.

Despite her flagging grades, she had managed to be accepted at a university, out of town. Jan moved into an all-female residence. Although her sexual response to females was as strong as ever, she was now extremely cautious about making friends. But she did befriend Lana, for whom she had an immediate affinity. One evening she and Lana were in her room, talking about the day's events. Jan felt an inexplicable surge of sadness coupled with a feeling of great warmth toward Lana. She felt she could trust her. Amid tears and trembling, she told Lana about her confused state, about her erotic response to women, about her horrid LB experience, about her promiscuity. She began to sob uncontrollably, and found herself being held by Lana, who at that moment seemed like the gentlest being whom Jan had ever touched.

They held each other until Jan's sobs began to subside and the tension in her body began to ease. Lana gently caressed Jan's hair and back, and began to kiss her. Jan allowed this to happen, and did not resist when Lana undressed her and made love to her.

Lana stayed with Jan for two or three hours, then left to return to her room. Jan's final orgasm had left her stunned and she fell into a deep sleep.

When Jan awoke the next morning, she was on an emotional rollercoaster, riding from joy to ecstasy to disgust and despair, to depression, then back to ecstasy again. What had just happened? She felt ashamed one moment, but the next moment she was warm all over lying there in pleasant reverie.

Jan didn't know whether to be angry at Lana for having taken advantage of her at a vulnerable moment or whether to embrace her for opening the door to her inner being. She decided to sit down with Lana to analyze what had happened.

Lana introduced Jan to the likelihood that she was a lesbian. Jan drew back from this possibility. How could she be? Hadn't she had intercourse with a hundred men? How could she be a lesbian? It wasn't right. It wasn't natural. And so on. Although she struggled with the idea, she experienced a flicker of hope that she might be on the road to discovering the real Jan, however rocky that road might be.

Jan began to read about homosexuality. She found herself getting closer to Lana, who had been an activist in a gay/lesbian community group in her home city. Jan attended group meetings for women who wanted to understand their sexuality better. Ultimately, Jan went into brief psychological counseling, which helped enormously in allowing her to come to grips with her homosexuality. One of the major tasks of the therapist was to dispel a myth to which Jan had clung: the myth that the sordid attempt at intercourse with the school hero was at the root of her sexual confusion and had "caused" her lesbianism.

Eventually, Jan came to understand that, regardless of the "reasons," she was a lesbian. Once she could accept that fact, she readjusted her thinking and her life accordingly. She acquired newfound confidence; she could stand in front of the mirror naked and alone, announcing to herself that she was worthy, free and the person she was. As she looked at the body she exalted in, a sense of pride overcame her. The most important conquest of her life was now complete—acceptance of herself.

Everything was clear now: Jan understood her response to LB, her promiscuous heterosexual behavior, the reason she had become so sexually aroused by the sight and smell of women. She understood, she accepted. Would her family and friends do the same?

Jan had grown up in a family that was open to discussion about practically anything and everything, including sex. Her parents knew that she had been on the birth-control pill and they suspected that she had been sexually active from her mid-teens onward. With so many boys in her life, they simply took for granted that she was sexually experienced. They never questioned her about it directly—they respected her privacy—but, from time to time, they spoke about sexually transmitted diseases and the need to practise safe sex.

Jan knew they had never thought for a moment that she was a lesbian. That fact made it more difficult for her to find the courage to tell them. Her older sister, Rebecca, was married, had a wonderful husband and a two-year-old daughter, and was pregnant again. Her pregnancy was the focus of the family's attention, as she was due within the next several weeks.

How could Jan come out to her parents now? She might have told Rebecca first, but Rebecca had only one thing on her mind at the moment. Jan felt paralyzed; she wanted to tell but simply could not.

Jan rehearsed in her mind every possible way of telling them and every possible response. In all of these coming-out vignettes, she pictured herself as the perpetrator of a crime, and her parents and Rebecca as the victims of it.

Jan's repertoire of scenarios was incomplete; missing was the possibility that her family would be totally accepting. This thought hadn't occurred to her. She was convinced that it was only "natural" for heterosexuals to be affronted by homosexuality. But Jan reflected again: Was she being fair to her parents? Jan had learned to understand herself, to accept herself, to be proud of herself. Perhaps she was underestimating the power of their love for her. Could her homosexuality diminish that love?

Jan told her parents simply and quickly—about LB, about her promiscuity, about her confusion, about Lana, about her psychological therapy. If they were stunned, if they were shocked, if they were disappointed, she never knew or saw it. Their response was immediate and clear. After hugging her to calm her anxiety and quiet her tears, they told her of their love for her and of their unshakeable support. A great calm had engulfed Jan. She was surprised at herself for thinking it would have happened in any other way.

• whose fault is it?

Not all families are as open and as understanding as Jan's. And not all the stories I've heard in my practice end as happily. I'll let Charlotte tell hers here.

"Dick and I had been married for twenty-four years when Andy told us he was gay. Until that point our marriage had been unbelievably strong; it had a fairy-tale quality to it. Dick and I were very much in love. He was a successful civil engineer, the owner of his own company. I was a social worker in a teaching hospital. We had it all: a home, two cars, a good income, one son and one daughter who were both excellent students. We lived in a small town where we knew everyone.

"My sexual life with Dick was extraordinary. He was a careful, patient, caring lover. We were both initiators. Sex was good all the time, but particularly outstanding on holidays. And then the bombshell—Andy's announcement. How things changed after that.

"Andy told me first. We were home alone. He said he couldn't tell Dick and asked me to do it. I was stunned. I didn't know what to do or say. It was as if Andy had taken a brush full of black paint and smeared it over the picture of our ideal family, sitting with our dog in front of the fireplace. I phoned Dick at work to come home immediately, which he did. I don't think that he said anything. He handled it in the way that he handled anything else—very quietly; he didn't get upset. In the meantime, I'm hysterical. I flew at Andy and attacked him. I asked him what we had ever done to him that he would do that to us. We didn't want our daughter, Sue, to hear us so the three of us got into the car and drove to the park. Andy was in the back seat of the car so he couldn't get out. When I think about it now I feel so upset with myself for treating Andy like a prisoner, like a piece of property that belongs to us, like a piece of furniture that belongs to us.

"Oh, he got an earful. I just couldn't understand it. Now I know it was naive of Dick and me. And here I am, a social worker, someone who's supposed to be supportive, empathetic. I could give that empathy to patients in the hospital, but not to my own son. Finally, I said to him that he had to see a psychiatrist. We have to get this fixed. That was the only thing that shut me up that night and allowed us to go home and go to bed when he said he would go. So he went.

"About two weeks later I said to him, 'How's it going with the psychiatrist?' He turned around and looked at me and he said, 'Mother, there is nothing wrong with me.' It just felt as if he took all of the power away from me and I didn't have any power anymore. He was in charge.

"Dick was bewildered. He just couldn't handle it. A new Dick emerged. Unrecognizable. I guess it's one thing to be liberal and it's another thing to be faced with reality. Not everybody will respond to reality in exactly the same way. Dick couldn't handle reality. He rejected the psychiatrist's view that Andy was normal. There has to be a cause, he kept saying over and over again. He kept going over and over again whatever details he could muster from Andy's upbringing. His behavior. My behavior. We must have done something wrong to lead Andy into this lifestyle. Dick was convinced it was a lifestyle that Andy had come to learn and, for whatever reason, found pleasure in. It was completely beyond him why anyone would enter a world of 'abnormality.'

"Didn't he have every privilege? Didn't he have everything he ever needed? Didn't we set an example of how a family should live together? Didn't all our friends in town see us as a perfect family? Dick became morose. He began to bark at me. Our sexual life deteriorated. I couldn't approach him. Our intimacy was evaporating. The more Andy demonstrated that he wasn't falling apart, that his life was moving on and that he was excelling in his chosen career pathway, the more hard-nosed and distant Dick became. Dick's view was that not only was Andy's behavior abnormal, but that he was reveling in it.

"One day Dick announced to me that he had finally analyzed the basis of Andy's homosexuality. My father had three brothers, two of whom had married and produced children. The third brother, Foster, had never married. He was a florist. Foster was a fancy dresser and he wore an overpowering man's cologne. He was my favorite uncle because of his good humor and easy way. He had frequently taken me and my sister on outings when we were children. He did the same with our kids. He adored them and they adored him. Dick saw it all now. It was crystal clear.

"Foster, he said, was gay—a 'faggot,' he called him, although he would never call his own son that. It was obvious. He never married, and what straight man would ever choose to become a florist, of all things. A florist? And he liked little children. Typical, Dick said. I couldn't believe what I was hearing. I had always pictured Dick as a sane, rational thinker. But there was more.

"Dick reasoned, if you can use that word, that Uncle Foster's influence came either directly through his personal contact or through the genes, he wasn't sure, and that I was the primary conduit through which Andy's homosexuality emerged. The evidence was plain to see, I was 'typically female,' with my hysterical outbursts, but yet he now accused me of being a smothering mother, often pushing aside his temperate, but firm more 'masculine' approach to matters. I was a social worker, a 'bleeding heart.' In my work I could be accepting of the most decrepit kind of person, even if that person was a homosexual dying of AIDS. The picture was complete. By example, and likely by genes, I was responsible for Andy's homosexuality. He could no longer be part of such a family.

"I was absolutely knocked off my feet. More stunned than when Andy came out. What had happened to our idyllic family? Where had I gone wrong. Yes, _I_. I searched within myself for an answer. Could Dick be right? Fortunately, that thought lasted for only a flash. Andy has taught me a lot; I also became a member of PFLAG. This group has taught me a lot; that's why you see me quoted in the newspapers and interviewed on TV. It's not a question of cause or blame. It's just the way it is. Dick just couldn't allow himself to see that. Once Dick got these notions into his head there was nothing I could do to reverse them. The divorce followed soon after."

• expected behavior

Dick is an extreme example of a person who refuses to change his views. But he is not alone. In every aspect of life, we are handed instructions on how to think, how to act, how to respond, how to feel. These "manuals" include views of what is right and what is wrong, what is good and what is bad, and are built upon myths that have become a meaningful part of our day-to-day existence.

What are the mythologies of our life everywhere around us? We construct our own or, more often, accept those projected by others since we consider the ones that are well established to be of proven credibility. Take our dress code. For many years society bought into the notion that, in order to be successful in life, it was necessary to dress in a particular fashion—suit and tie for a businessman, for example. Why does the businessman *have* to dress this way? We have created the mythical notion that this is the "proper" way to dress to enhance business, to receive promotions. Why can't he dress some other way? in jeans and a sweatshirt, say? Will he suddenly become inarticulate, ineffectual? According to the myth, he won't be as readily accepted if he dresses casually (other than on Friday). He'll lose business. He won't get promoted. Fortunately for all of us, we are shedding this myth, albeit slowly.

Mythologies pervade our life. Every religion has created its own rules and codes of behavior, all based on specific perceptions of the nature of the world.

We also live by a collection of do's and don'ts, of rights and wrongs, traceable to cultural traditions, to edicts from on high. Courteous men allow women to precede them, open the door for women, give up seats for them, carry their parcels. Why?

Because such behavior is proper and genteel. It's the "right" thing to do. This circular reasoning is a part of many of our mythologies.

If we were to keep asking Why? about every expected kind of behavior or every expected mode of thinking, the answer we'd hear most often would be: *tradition,* even if that tradition had ceased to carry any logic with it. That same answer applies to our view of sexual orientation, for, in the end, there is no persuasive reason why the way another person conducts his or her sexual life (as long as it is not hurtful) has any bearing on us.

Our mythologies provide us with emotional and social stability. If we know how to act, how to respond, in a wide variety of circumstances, we are less anxious, because we are at one with the others in our lives who share our packaged view of existence.

These packages are created by our parents, our friends, our bosses, our religious institutions, our radio and television and books. We are constantly being bombarded with the "right" way to think, to behave, to act under each and every circumstance. And we generally acquiesce, accepting those packages which give us a sense of identity, a sense of belonging. No one wants to be isolated, to be seen as different.

But people *are* different. Each of us is a free, independent human entity. As the philosopher Jean-Paul Sartre said, we are "condemned to be free." If that is so, then we are ultimately responsible for our actions. We have no one else to fall back on, to blame. If we are free, we can think this way or that way about the nature of things. We think that we relinquish our freedom when we let others do our thinking for us; but even that is an expression of our freedom, because we have freely chosen to acquiese. We can't escape our freedom, but we can escape from a particular thought or behavior. We can *act* in a different way.

• a lesson in prejudice

Take a look at the prejudices in your own family. Your twenty-three-year-old daughter, Dini, is bright and outgoing. You've brought her up with what you consider high moral standards, to respect others and to expect to receive respect herself. Through your example, she has learned to be concerned about others and has translated this into direct action. Your church's social action committee has taken on a project to help the homeless. You have made a generous financial donation to this project and have provided two boxes of clothing. You have just cause to feel good about yourself and to feel proud of Dini's active involvement. She and other committee members prepare and serve one meal a week at a nearby shelter for destitute men and women.

One day Dini announces that she and one of her fellow committee members, Edward, have struck up a close friendship and she would like to invite him home for supper. She hinted this was a serious relationship but she felt she wanted her parents to meet him before she announced intentions of commitment. The two of you are delighted. What could be better? A young man for your daughter with not only the same religious persuasion but with a similar philosophy of concern for the less privileged.

Edward arrives on the appointed night. He rings the door-bell. When he enters the living room, there is a moment of stunned silence. Dini has neglected to tell you that Edward's racial heritage is different from yours.

The great liberal tradition in your family has met an unexpected challenge. Your extended hand says welcome and stay, your heart says please go away.

You're courteous through the meal. You're respectful. But you're already thinking, planning what you're going to say to Dini when she says: well, what do you think? She should have told you of his heritage? But why? What difference would that have made? Would you have told her not to bring him home for dinner?

Sometimes our prejudices are obvious, overt, apparent to us and to others. Sometimes they're hidden, subtle, covert. Sometimes they're put to the test. For the most part, thankfully, they're not. Dini is a free independent woman, it's her life. But what about us? Don't we count?

A short and quick answer? When it comes right down to it—no!

Despite all the pre-packaged mythologies that surround us, we are free to deliberate and make choices. We are free to accept another view of our world. We are free to explore many things, including sexuality, in ways we have not yet imagined. Sexuality is part of our humanity. Some accepted mythologies package sexuality as an assortment of stereotypes that stand as barriers to understanding—not only others, but also ourselves.

chapter six

• what "causes" homosexuality?

Our traditional way of thinking about sexual orientation is very static. We are either heterosexual (our erotic preference is the opposite sex), homosexual (we are sexually attracted to the same sex), or we are bisexual (we are sexually attracted to both sexes). The conventional notion is that our orientation is fixed and that, under normal circumstances, our behavior is exclusively consistent with our orientation. This may well be correct. But, some will argue, it may not be necessarily so.

We can understand homosexual explorations of children and adolescents who are beginning to learn about their own sexuality and are beginning to understand what it means to be sexual with another human being. We can understand the homosexual behavior of those in prison or at war, situations in which one is deprived of a sexual outlet in what may well be the preferred mode, the mode of "true" sexual orientation, the heterosexual mode. We can understand the lesbian love of two older heterosexual women who simply cannot find a suitable male lover and soulmate but have found each other.

We believe that, in ordinary circumstances, these individuals would not have engaged in behavior that runs counter to their "true," innate sexual orientation or preference. We believe this because conventional wisdom makes sense to us. But reality may be more complicated. Are we all, in fact, somewhere on a line between exclusive heterosexuality and exclusive homosexuality? Does our place on that line change according to variations in our belief system, in the conventional wisdom, in societal attitudes?

We have two attributes to consider: (1) sexual feelings, desire, orientation, preference—the sex we actually prefer our sexual partner to be; and (2) behavior—what we actually do. Some say that preference is fixed by genetics or some other biological factor; some say that preference is flexible, molded by environmental factors that themselves are changeable and subject to the influences of culture and history. If homosexuality is really a matter of environmental influence, rather than biological necessity, then we should be able to find ways to offset the environmental influences and have a homosexual individual revert to heterosexuality. If, on the other hand, homosexuality is fixed at birth by a genetic or hormonal malfunction, or some traumatic event in intrauterine life, then we must simply accept it (since we have no other choice). But, by believing this, are we also accepting the idea that homosexuality is a deviation from normalcy, like so many other conditions? And, in so doing, do we then look upon homosexuality as a "medical condition" that requires study and the development of therapeutic strategies to deal with it? Many thinking parents struggle with these sorts of questions on learning their child is gay.

Let us explore some of the "causation" theories and see where they lead us.

• is it biology?

If homosexuality is a medical condition, an abnormality, then it must have a "cause" or "causes." Is there a gene that determines heterosexuality? How powerful is that gene? Is there a different gene for men and for women? Does it always work? What happens if that gene is totally absent? Does the individual then become homosexual or have no sexual inclination whatsoever? What happens if there is a mutation in the heterosexuality gene? Is an individual with a mutated gene heterosexual with homosexual inclinations? Does everybody have a heterosexuality and homosexuality gene, and is it just a matter of the relative balance between the two that determines our ultimate sexual orientation? The genetic questions are endless.

There has been extensive research into the biological and sociological foundations from which homosexual desire emerges, but scholars in this area of scientific endeavor have reached no firm conclusions.

Biological studies have been approached from a number of different perspectives. The majority of these studies have been undertaken in males only. Highlights of the major biological approaches are summarized below.

1. hormones

The most obvious area to consider is the role hormones play in sexual identity. Hormones are chemical substances produced by endocrine glands in the body. These glands (pituitary, thyroid, parathyroid, adrenal, pancreas, ovaries, testes, etc.) produce these chemical substances, which are then secreted into the bloodstream. The hormones go to particular distant sites to perform their specific functions.

The hormonal influences on sexual behavior come from three important locations: the hypothalamus, the pituitary gland, and the gonads (testes in men, ovaries in women). The hypothalamus is part of the lower structure of the brain. It has many functions including the production of gonadotropin-releasing hormone (GnRH), which goes to the pituitary gland, the master gland of the body. The pituitary gland hangs down from the base of the brain, immediately below the hypothalamus, and produces a variety of hormones that either stimulate the action of other glands or have direct effects on various bodily functions such as growth, or milk production during nursing.

Under the stimulus of GnRH, the pituitary gland, in turn, produces two sex hormones: follicle-stimulating hormone (FSH) and lutenizing hormone (LH). In women these stimulate the ovaries to produce female sex hormones and to cause the release of eggs. In men, LH and FSH go to the testes to stimulate male sex hormone (testosterone) production, and to initiate sperm production. Testosterone as well as female sex hormones, such as estradiol and progesterone, are produced in both males and females. Testosterone predominates in males; estradiol predominates in females. Certain bodily changes can occur if the balance between the male and female sex hormones is even slightly askew.

Scientists have long been interested in studying the effects of the sex hormones on behavior. Most often studied are the behavioral effects of testosterone. Testosterone is a very potent aphrodisiac; that is, it stimulates the sex drive in both males and females. It is not the only factor responsible for sexual arousal, but it is perhaps the most significant one. As a result, abnormalities in testosterone production have been sought in a spectrum of circumstances, including sexual orientation.

Many studies of groups of gay men have measured blood hormone levels, especially the level of testosterone. The hormonal theory of sexual orientation in men holds that a lower-than-normal level of testosterone is associated with homosexual behavior. In each of the many studies reported in the literature, hormones were measured in the blood and the average levels in the homosexual and heterosexual groups were compared. The results of all these studies fall into three completely different groups. Homosexual men were found to have: (1) lower; (2) higher; or (3) the same level of testosterone as straight men. Thus there is no conclusive evidence that there is any hormonal difference between the two groups of men. My colleagues Dr. Ron Langevin and Dr. Michael Sanders and I undertook one such study and found no differences between straight and gay men.

Perhaps exposure of the developing fetus to particular hormones may induce a behavioral imprint in the hypothalamus or other brain parts that, in later life, predisposes a person to a particular kind of sexual orientation. Or this imprint may occur very early in childhood. The evidence that this occurs, however, is not very compelling.

2. size of the hypothalamus

As indicated above, the hypothalamus, located at the base of the brain, above the pituitary gland, is involved in a number of hormonal and metabolic control mechanisms, such as sex-

hormone action and emotional responses. In 1991, in a prestigious medical journal, *Science*, Simon LeVay, a brain researcher,
published the results of a study that claimed to show that a key
portion of the hypothalamus was a different size in homosexual
as compared to heterosexual men. LeVay did post-mortem
studies on the hypothalami of forty-one men by means of a very
sensitive body-imaging technique known as "positron emission
tomography "(PET) scan. Nineteen of the forty-one were
homosexual men who had died of AIDS. He found that the
hypothalami of the gay men were significantly smaller than
those of the straight men. In fact, they were approximately the
same size as the hypothalami of women. The sexual orientation
of females whose hypothalami were studied in this manner is
not known.

So here we have a suggestion that a crucial part of the brain
of homosexual men is significantly different in size from the
same structure in heterosexual men. Does this really mean that
this apparent difference represents the basis for male homosexuality? Far from it. First, the results of one study can never be
taken as final, since the study may contain methodological
errors or biases. Studies of this nature have to be done repeat-
edly by different groups around the world; that is, they have to
be duplicated or reproduced, by other scientists to verify that
the methodology is sound, and that there were no biases in the
analysis of the data and the interpretation of the results. These
validating studies have not yet been undertaken.

Even if we accepted LeVay's findings as being true for all gay
men as compared with straight men, we would have to be sure
that we could explain the results and defend them against
significant criticism of their interpretation. LeVay's study is

open to several interpretations. One is that it could have been the AIDS and not the homosexual state that caused a decrease in the size of the hypothalamus in the gay men. Another possible explanation is that the smaller hypothalamus was a *consequence* of the homosexuality of the subjects rather than a *cause* of it. LeVay's research is interesting but cannot be taken as producing an immutable truth.

3. genetics

Is homosexuality actually passed on through the generations by some form of genetic factor? Several types of studies have been done that suggest these factors exist.

One of the techniques used to determine the influence of genetics on physical or behavioral traits is the study of twins (identical or monozygotic, splitting of one fertilized egg; fraternal or dizygotic, two fertilized eggs), as compared with non-twin siblings. The theory holds that genetic factors are at play if the characteristics under study are most common in a group of monozygotic twins, less common but still common in dizygotic twins, and least common in a group of non-twin siblings.

This is exactly what has been found in a number of studies that look at the incidence of homosexuality in families of homosexual men. J.M. Bailey and R.C. Pillard, for example, recruited homosexual men who had a monozygotic twin, a dizygotic twin brother or an adopted brother. They found that 52 percent of the monozygotic brothers, 22 percent of the dizygotic brothers, and 11 percent of the adoptive brothers were homosexual. Unfortunately, in this study, not every one of the brothers could be asked directly about his sexual orientation.

Since the original homosexual subject's report on this matter provided the information, the findings were somewhat questionable. This is a particular methodological problem with this particular study, but all studies of this nature have their methodological problems, making it extremely difficult to form firm conclusions about factors that may lead to homosexuality.

It could be argued, for example, that homosexuality occurs more frequently in monozygotic twins, not because of genetic factors, but because of social factors. Some might say that there is much closer bonding between identical twins, who look exactly alike, than between fraternal twins, who may resemble each other but do not look alike. The bonding with a non-twin brother, although possibly strong, might still not be as powerful as that shared between monozygotic or dizygotic twins. If this is the case, then, if homosexuality is really a consequence of social or environmental factors rather than genetic ones, the socially closer identical twins might tend to be more alike than siblings in other kinds of relationships.

All of this is speculation, of course, but it does illustrate the great difficulty in coming up with one irrefutable interpretation of results of scientific experimentation. The Bailey and Pillard data, for example, have not been reliably replicated. In fact, at least one other study found a far lower concordance rate for homosexuality among identical twins.

Despite all of these musings about "causes," the nature of the research, the motivation behind the research and the interpretation of the research, one fact remains: An individual's sexual orientation is what it is. Whether it is biologically induced, whether it is a matter of rearing, whether it is a deliberate choice or whether it is changeable, parents cannot influence it, but can only accept or reject it.

In a democratic society, we don't discriminate (or should not) against individuals on the basis of how they vote, on the basis of their religion or their color or any other aspect of a life that is conducted in accordance with laws that don't affirm the right of the majority to tyrranize the minority. We will be what we will be. Our children will be what they will be. If society is uncomfortable with that, it is society that needs changing, not our children.

There are those who argue that sexual orientation is a continuum between exclusive homosexuality and exclusive heterosexuality. Is our sexuality really so rigidly defined? Or can our position on that continuum change under certain circumstances? These questions are not asked in relation to our behavior, which we know is changeable, but with regard to our inner feelings and the sexual attractiveness with which others excite us. Given free choice and the mandate to exercise that choice, would we choose a male or female sexual partner?

There may be no simple answer to that question, and we must recognize that, for many, if not most, individuals, sexual orientation is fixed and efforts to deny it, suppress it, or alter it can lead to devastating consequences.

• Eric's struggle

Eric had difficulty articulating his major complaints when he first visited my office. This is how he expressed himself: "I feel empty. . . . There's no life, actually. . . . I live but that's about it. . . . I enjoy nothing—it's numb, dead; there's nothing there."

Eric, fifty-five, had been married almost thirty years. They had one child several years into the marriage. After this child was born, Eric developed erectile dysfunction and, because he and his wife had intercourse very infrequently, they thought they would have no more children. But a second child came along some two years later. For the last twenty years, they had not had intercourse because Eric was unable to achieve an erection.

Now Eric entertained thoughts of suicide. He had fantasies of driving into a telephone pole or jumping out of the window of a highrise building. He had reached his wits' end, driven there by despair about the meaning of his life and the meaning of his sexuality.

When Eric was a child, he knew he was somehow different from the men in his life. The heterosexual men around him had girl friends, wives and female lovers. To him this seemed unnatural, although he didn't quite understand why. The reason became clear when, at age sixteen, he was approached by a married man who lived next door with his wife and children and asked to perform fellatio. Eric then knew why he and his neighbor were different from the other men in Eric's life. This was an activity that gave Eric intense pleasure, so intense that he and his neighbor entered into a relationship that lasted three years. Eric finally felt compelled to leave home before his family discovered his secret.

During his teen years, he also experimented on several occasions with other teenage boys, but he felt he could never publicly acknowledge his homosexuality. He couldn't even acknowledge it to himself in any meaningful way.

When he left home, he became celibate. He was approached many times by men, but the idea of continuing to have sexual relations with men made him uncomfortable. He had grown up with the idea that homosexuality was a sin. Eric spent a lot of time crying; he did not know what to do. After meeting the woman who was to become his wife, he felt that his only escape was to try to normalize his life by getting married.

For thirty years Eric had lived with the despair of not knowing who he was. He wanted normalcy but didn't know how to acquire it, where to find it. He had seen psychiatrists in the past to discuss his erectile dysfunction, but his underlying anguish was never dealt with; his sexual orientation did not appear on the psychiatrists' agendas. The only way Eric felt he could cope with his confusion was by retreating into an alcoholic haze. For the last 10 years he would drink about 7 litres of wine per week.

When Eric sought help now, after all these years, saying: "I enjoy nothing—it's numb, dead; there's nothing there." The diagnosis was obvious. Eric was depressed.

What Eric desperately needed, and what he got, was therapy for his depression that did not gloss over the fact that he was gay. Even before his first meeting with the psychiatrist Eric seemed to have a lighter demeanor. He understood that he was gay and that the therapy was not going to try to "convert" him into being straight, but was going to help him come to terms with who he really was and to live in serenity with that persona. Will therapy succeed at this stage of his life? This answer depends on what the measure of success is, but there is reason to be optimistic.

Eric is gay. He tried to suppress this self-evident fact because he knew it didn't fit the expectations of his family, his culture and, ultimately, himself. But he is only now learning that, at age fifty-five, after having tried to "normalize" himself by marrying a woman and having children. How much more sensible his life would have been had he been able, from childhood onward, to allow the real Eric to live.

• is it environment?

The person we come to be at any one stage in our life (and that person is constantly evolving) is a product of our genetic makeup, the influence of our environment and a combination of both elements. Genetic factors either make themselves immediately apparent, such as our sex or the color of our eyes, or appear only in the presence of positive environmental stimuli (e.g., enough nutrition to reach our genetically determined height) or negative environmental stimuli (e.g., smoking, which activates cancer-producing genes). Genetic traits are fixed, but what we learn from the environment can be unlearned.

If this is the case, many argue, and if homosexuality is environmentally induced, as many believe, then homosexuality is learned and can be unlearned. Homosexuals, therefore, can be converted to heterosexuality through some form of therapeutic process. What environmental influences could induce homosexuality?

Many parents believe that sexual orientation can be affected by traumatic events in their children's lives. Consider the story of Enid.

• Enid's trauma

Enid was twenty-two years old when she finally said enough is enough. She had been dating since age fifteen; she first had sexual intercourse at age seventeen. At nineteen she became pregnant and had a therapeutic abortion. In retrospect, none of the intercourse she experienced provided her with the sexual ecstasy she thought sex was supposed to bring. She did experience an emotional high during her brief pregnancy but realized that pregnancy was not at all a realistic state for her to be in at this stage of her life.

She had always had warm feelings for her many girl friends, but never in a sexual way, at least until one January night when she was twenty. She and her girl friend Joy had just had dinner and shared a bottle of wine. They sat down on the couch together to watch TV. Enid, not much of a wine drinker, stretched out on the couch, covered up with a blanket, and drifted, half asleep, half awake. Joy got up and cleared the table. Enid fell asleep but awoke dreamily about thirty minutes later. She saw Joy undressing prior to having a shower and Enid became aroused. A rush of sexual electricity went through her as she watched Joy neatly fold her clothes and head for the shower, completely unaware of Enid's auto-erotic experience.

Enid never approached Joy in a sexual manner. She knew that Joy was heterosexual and she didn't want to jeopardize their friendship. In fact, after that evening, Enid did not approach any woman in a sexual context. What she did do was go to a counseling centre to talk to someone about her experiences. She didn't know she was a lesbian, and she didn't want to be one, but that episode in Joy's apartment told her that this issue needed to be explored.

Enis found her subsequent dates with men to be less and less satisfying. She found that she was increasingly turned off by sexual intercourse with men. One or two homosexual experiences convinced her of her sexual orientation. With further reading and participation in group discussions with other lesbians she came to understand what her sexual preference was. At age twenty-two she told her parents.

Her parents were taken aback but didn't withdraw from her. They wanted to understand, to help her, to support her. But they also wanted to know why. They bombarded Enid with questions, searching for the "cause." When she told them about the pregnancy, they both said, "That's it." They argued that, because the pregnancy had been unwanted, Enid had turned against men and, instead, sought the companionship of women, with whom she could have sexual activity without becoming pregnant. Since Enid "learned" how to become a lesbian, she could just as well unlearn it through therapy. Of course, therapy didn't change a thing. Enid still preferred sex with women.

Her parents were beside themselves. They sat Enid down and implored her to think back: "Enid, there must be something that happened when you were a teenager, or a child, that turned you in this direction." There *was* something that Enid had never told them. She could hardly contain her tears as she recounted the sexual abuse she had suffered from age four to six at the hands of a teenage male babysitter. She recalled how, after forcing her to manually bring him to orgasm, he would take her to the bathroom to wash her hands.

Finally, her parents thought, now we've got it. Such an experience would turn any woman off men and lead her into the arms of a woman who could offer solace and comfort. Enid reluctantly returned to therapy and achieved relief from the pain and anxiety of the suppressed memory of childhood abuse, but she emerged with the same erotic preference.

Twenty years later, Enid's parents are still anguished and angry that psychiatry failed to rid Enid of the devastating emotional effect of the abuse and, instead, "caused" her to turn to lesbianism. But they are wrong.

Enid, a successful author, has never been able to bring her female partner of eighteen years to her parents' home. With both anger and compassion toward her parents, Enid has been unable to achieve complete happiness in her life. Having imposed on herself the need for parental blessing, she recognizes that her disappointment is of her own making, the failure to meet an expectation over which she has no control.

• some outdated theories

What about the possibility of psychological or social factors, or a combination of both, being at the root of gay or lesbian orientation? For years, a series of psychosocial theories have been proposed that purport to explain the homosexual drive. Such theories argue that, if a certain set of social conditions prevails, the sexual orientation of an individual experiencing those conditions will be predictable. These types of inquiries have occupied the attention of researchers for many years. What has been the outcome? Well, if the results of the biological studies are somewhat murky, those emerging from psychosocial inquiries are a veritable quagmire.

Some of these theories seem like fanciful flights of imagination or wishful thinking not only on the part of the researchers, but also on the part of a large sector of the public that is desperate to find an explanation for a form of sexual orientation they cannot understand.

If these theories are old and outmoded, why include them in this book? It is important to examine them for the purpose of dismissing them. Each one of them will have been seized upon in desperation by parents, families, friends, workmates and acquaintances of gay men and women—"Oh, he's gay because he's afraid of women, or because he has a dominant mother and a wimpy father, or because his mother babied and pampered him." "She's lesbian because of an abusive father, or sexual abuse, or a negative sexual experience, or an unwanted pregnancy." The fabricated cause-and-effect relationships are endless when armchair "psychologists" are at work, some well-intentioned, some malicious, all wreaking havoc.

1. aversion to females

This theory holds that closeness to women can cause such a level of anxiety in some men that they prefer not to be in the company of women, particularly if there is a sexual connotation to their interaction. This is not a very convincing proposition, first, because homosexual men are not primarily interested in sexual activity with women and might, indeed, become anxious if thrust into that situation, and, secondly, and of far greater significance, because homosexual men often relate extremely well to women, with whom they can develop a close camaraderie.

2. narcissism

The narcissistic person's primary focus is him- or herself. Not only is the narcissist self-centered, but he or she also derives sexual pleasure from him- or herself. A same-sex partner is a stand-in for the narcissist's true love object, his or her own body. The most intense narcissism, say some psychoanalysts, therefore, leads to homosexuality. There is no proof of this.

3. male partners as surrogate females

This theory holds that gay men really have an erotic preference for females, but, because of a debilitating anxiety about having sex with a female, they turn to other men for sex because men are perceived as less threatening. It's fascinating how some psychoanalysts have been able to manipulate Sigmund Freud's theories of sexual development.

There are well-known situations, however, in which heterosexual men (whose preferred sexual object is female) do use other men as surrogate females by having sex with them. These sexual acts occur in situations of deprivation, such as in prisons or on long sea voyages, where there are no women present. In these circumstances, some men are able to have sex with other men while fantasizing that they are with a woman.

4. female gender identity

All of us perceive ourselves as male or female and adopt a role in acting out that perception. One of the theories of male homosexuality holds that gay men are more feminine, have a stronger female gender identity, than heterosexual men. In a paper entitled "Feminine Gender Identity in Homosexual Men: How Common Is It?" Dr. Michael Sanders and Dr. Ron Langevin, and I addressed this very question. The men studied, both homosexual and heterosexual, were part of the research we conducted at the University of Toronto. We investigated a number of factors, both hormonal and psychosocial, in the two groups of men. One of the items tested was gender identity.

Gender identity is not the same as gender role. With each passing decade, gender roles are becoming less and less distinct. Activities that were once the exclusive domain of men or of women are more and more being done by members of both sexes. Cooking is no longer exclusively the domain of women, nor is hockey exclusively the domain of men. Housekeeping is no longer the domain of women, and woodworking is no longer the domain of men. Practising medicine is no longer exclusively a male domain, and nursing is no longer exclusively for women. And so it goes. Distinct gender roles have not disappeared altogether, but they have certainly changed and are no longer a significant influence in how human beings act.

Gender identity, however, is generally quite firmly fixed throughout life (some notable examples exist in the medical literature where this is not the case). By and large, men identify themselves quite clearly as males, and women identify themselves quite clearly as females, irrespective of their roles in society and their behavioral patterns. Some individuals, though, do express ambivalence, or uncertainty about their gender identity, and feel as if they have a male and female component to their psyche. Others, transsexuals, feel that nature has robbed them of the appropriate physical exterior, their true gender identity. Many of these individuals will persist in their determination to undergo a sex-reversal operation to achieve the right body for their psyche and the gender identity with which they have gone through life.

• Victoria: gay or straight?

When Vance was five years old, he had this irresistible urge to put on his mother's lipstick and prance around in his mother's shoes. His parents thought it was cute and didn't pay much attention to it. When Vance was seven, and still playing with his sister's dolls, his father became a little concerned and made sure that Vance had more than enough "boys'" toys to keep him occupied. Despite the trucks and the baseball mitt and the erector set, Vance still gravitated toward the play kitchen and pretended to cook up a storm, "just like Mommy."

Vance's dad died when he was ten. With his mother at work and his sister at her ballet lessons, Vance had a field day in his mother's closet, trying on everything. It gave him a tingle to see himself in front of the mirror dressed as a female.

At age twelve, Vance discovered male magazines that displayed men in all sorts of poses, with all sorts of muscles, both with and without clothes. Vance began to masturbate regularly while perusing these magazines. He had no interest in female magazines, nor did he have an interest in having sex with a female. His sexual attraction was exclusively toward men.

But there was something unusual about this attraction. Vance always fantasized that the men were penetrating him, entering a vagina. He never imagined himself penetrating these magazine men. As a matter of fact, he was somewhat revolted by the fact that he had a penis at all. Where his penis was, there should have been a vagina. He was also attracted to men's chests and imagined that they found his chest—one he imagined had female breasts—appealing as well. Vance realized that he was sexually attracted to men as a female would be and wanted them to be sexually attracted to him as a female. Nature had robbed him, giving him a female psyche and a male body. This had to be changed.

When Vance was nineteen, he could no longer stand to act out his life as a male. Despite his body, he was a female and that's how he wanted the world to know him. That's how he wanted to have sex, heterosexually, with a male partner.

Vance became Victoria. As Victoria, he went to a university gender clinic for psychological support. Victoria fulfilled the clinic's requirements in preparation for the sex-reversal operation she knew she must have. Regardless of the cost, she would eventually have whatever medical and surgical procedures were necessary in order to fulfill what she now realized was a lifelong dream: to become fully and completely female. She understood she would never bear children, but at least her body would match her psyche.

Vance/Victoria represents a classic case of the male-to-female transsexual. Female-to-male transsexuals have an analogous frustration. Outwardly they are one gender; inwardly they have the feelings and identity of the opposite gender. Many transsexuals strive to change their exterior because their interior is unchangeable. Are transsexuals homosexuals? On the surface, it would seem they are, but the majority are heterosexual, since the object of their sexual desire is someone whose body may look like theirs, but whose gender identity matches that body. A small number of transsexuals are homosexually oriented; in other words, a male-to-female transsexual is attracted to a woman, and a female-to-male transsexual is attracted to a man. Homosexual transsexuals are a distinct minority.

What about gay men? Did they acquire a female gender identity, presumably early in life, with the result that their more female psyche naturally led them to have a homosexual erotic preference? Or, conversely, if they were homosexual to begin with, did their homosexuality result in a reduction in male gender identity and an increase in female gender identity? This is the old chicken-and-egg dilemma revisited.

The results of our study showed that homosexual men were not female-identified; gender identity and sexual orientation are not likely to be causally related; homosexual men have a clear masculine gender identity that, on average, is less intense than that of heterosexual men.

There is one important point to make here. There is a clear difference between feminine gender identity, as discussed above, and feminine behavior. Many men, whether homosexual or heterosexual, enjoy activities that society has traditionally labeled as feminine, but both these group of men retain their unequivocal sense of themselves as males; that is, they have a clear male gender identity. This is as true of effeminate men as it is of non-effeminate men.

5. disturbed parent–child relationships

A popular idea that was promoted in the research literature and that is still prevalent today among parents who discover that one or more of their children is gay or lesbian is that there was some sort of disturbance or anomaly in the way they reared their child. There may have, indeed, been a disturbance or anomaly in the process of rearing, but was that interaction the "cause" of their child's homosexuality?

There is a common belief that, in childhood gay men had a close relationship with their mothers and a poor relationship with their fathers. Some studies have shown that this set of circumstances existed, but it is not universal among gay men, and, therefore, cannot be considered a determining factor in the child's ultimate sexual orientation. No studies provide unequivocal evidence for any specific aspects of child rearing as precursors to homosexual preference.

6. homosexuality as a learned phenomenon

Many workers in the field of sexual studies have argued that homosexuality is a consequence of having learned to prefer homosexual orgasmic release early in life or at the outset of sexual experiences with others. Such learning occurs, so the theory goes, when a young boy is seduced by an older boy or man. There is little evidence to support the theory that homosexuality is learned. One has only to pay attention to the anecdotal evidence from gay men to conclude that there is no consistent early-learning pattern.

If, according to the learning theory, all boys are basically heterosexual and become homosexual only through some form of learning experience, then one would expect that treatment to unlearn the behavior would be effective. Therapy based on behavior modification should return the individual to his "appropriate" heterosexual state. Despite the voluminous literature on therapeutic attempts to change gay men into straight men, there is very little evidence to suggest that erotic preference can be altered. This observation significantly weakens the theory that learning is a factor in homosexuality.

Should we even attempt "treatment" to convert a homosexual man into a heterosexual one? For parents who believe that a homosexual child can be converted to a heterosexual one, I offer the answer that Ron Langevin, in *Sexual Strands*, provides:

> A homosexual does not choose to have an erotic preference for men any more than heterosexuals can choose to prefer women. Homosexual men represent the full gamut of human personality and talents, from poets and scientists to ministers of church and state to labourers and mechanics. To have their whole life degenerated because they are homosexual seems like poor therapeutic practice.

Looking for "causes" of homosexuality is a fruitless and frustrating endeavor. Although it is part of being human to constantly raise questions and seek answers, with respect to homosexuality why do we care so much? What difference does it make? Sexual orientation is a private matter. How we construct our lives is a private matter as long as we don't infringe upon the rights of others. The great philosopher Bertrand Russell put it this way: "The freedom we seek is not the right to oppress others, but the right to live as we choose and think as we choose, where our doing so does not prevent others from doing likewise."

III

accepting your gay child

chapter seven

• religious attitudes

When someone close to you—a son or daughter, a parent, a sibling—is trying to tell you something that is troubling, speaking with hesitancy, or anxiety, or fear, or pain, having great difficulty finding the right words, how do you respond? Do you get up and walk away? Do you urge your loved ones to hurry up and speak their mind? Do you wait patiently until they find the right words? Sometimes we tell others secrets about ourselves because we hope that, in the telling, we can experience a sense of relief or share the burden of our secret.

But some secrets are too much to bear, weigh too heavily on our psyche, on our every breathing moment. Even if we know that revealing the secret might bring dire consequences, we still feel anxious about not sharing some important things particularly with our family, those closest to us, our loved ones.

• Ed's burden
Ed, at age twenty-nine, felt such a burden. He had carried the secret of his sexuality with him, alone, for too many years.

Ed was an intelligent, tough-minded, strong-willed man. He had made mistakes, and he knew what he had to do to correct them. Ed had been married to Janet for three years, and the marriage was not working. He felt stifled, not able to be himself; their sexual life was abysmal. Finally, Ed told Janet he was gay, and the marriage came to an abrupt end. As they had no children, the separation and divorce would be relatively easy.

Ed had been untrue to himself, and certainly untrue to Janet. He spoke to me about his dilemma.

• being true to yourself

"I knew I was gay when we married. From the age of thirteen to my university years, I had had sexual activity exclusively with the same male partner. Prior to my marriage, I had had sexual encounters with an additional four men. But marriage to a woman seemed the right thing to do, seemed appropriate for a professional man, an accountant, with aspirations of working in the corporate world. It also seemed appropriate from my religious upbringing. My faith taught several fundamental principles: First, marriage is a fulfillment of God's divine masterplan for the human race. Through marriage, sexual contact is sanctified, particularly for the purpose of having a family. The Bible does say, 'Go forth and multiply.' I was certainly expected to do this, and I expected it of myself. Second, my religion views homosexuality as an abomination. I had already engaged in gay sex and thought marriage to a woman would end that practice. I seriously questioned the wisdom of entering into a heterosexual marriage, knowing that my sexual preference was totally male-directed. But I thought I could do it, especially since Janet was an extraordinarily fine woman: intelligent, beautiful, humorous, kind and giving. But it didn't work. I was untrue both to myself and to Janet. I lived the lie for three years, but I couldn't live it any longer. Telling Janet was relatively easy; I had to tell her. After the telling, we would separate and likely have no further contact. But telling my parents was another story.

Despite the inner strength for which I had always prided myself, despite my self-assurance, I was apprehensive about telling my mother and father something that they did not at all want to hear. I would have to tell them about my separation from Janet, whom my parents had come to love as their own daughter, and I would have to tell the reason why."

Ed steeled himself, even though he had always had a free and easy relationship with his parents. He was anxious nonetheless.

His parents were visibly upset, but they didn't "go off the deep end," as Ed put it. As hurt as they were, they affirmed their respect for Ed's right to his own personhood. They were undeniably saddened about losing Janet, who had become part of their world. They wanted to reach out to her, and they did— and to her parents.

Tom and Erma reminded themselves their son, their flesh and blood, had just told them one of the most important, most heart-wrenching facts about his life. They knew he had been tense and anxious, and even afraid, as they were now.

Tom and Erma also knew that Ed really needed their support at this trying moment. They wanted to give him that support but they could not face this alone. They had to talk to someone, so they turned to their minister, expecting to hear words of hope and consolation, for emotional guidance and a message of inspiration. But their minister was imprisoned by his own rhetoric. The only words he came up with were *tragedy, misfortune, sin, abomination, punishment* and *prayer*. He didn't understand their anguish. He had a message to deliver and that message didn't coincide with the real need of the moment. His view was that the Bible was clear on this issue. Every effort should be made to exorcise Ed. He would pray for them.

Tom and Erma were staunch members of the church. They and Ed had participated enthusiastically in church activities, and the church had always been there for them. It didn't seem to be there for them now. They were skeptical about psychological therapy and wondered if they had their own resources to deal with this. They turned to Ed to help them.

Tom and Erma were bright, intelligent people who needed time to understand, to absorb the impact of the news their son had delivered. They had questions, concerns. They talked over their concerns with Ed and ultimately they were able to express their unconditional support of him.

Ed's partner entered the picture shortly thereafter. He joined the family, just as Janet had done previously. Ed's sister and brother-in-law were soon able to get past their initial discomfort. Soon Ed's homosexuality became a non-issue for the entire family.

Ed is a lucky man. He is able to lead a normal life. His entire family has accepted him as he is and he and his partner live a normal life with the love and support of Ed's extended family.

While Tom and Erma had grown up in the church and knew what the church's attitude toward homosexuality was, they believed there was some latitude, some room for compassion, in the dogma. It wasn't even possible to think otherwise. Their view was that the church didn't fail them, but their minister did.

• the rejected daughter

Rahani was not as lucky as Ed. By the age of fifteen, she knew that she had no interest in boys and that she would never marry. Although she had not yet had a sexual encounter, she knew that, when she did, it would be with another girl or woman.

Rahani was faithful to her family and to her religion in the acts of daily life. A dutiful daughter, she readily accepted the responsibilities she was given. She never told anyone about her homoerotic feelings, but she knew that one day there would be a family crisis when she would refuse to be party to an arranged marriage. In her country, culture and religion, arranged marriages were the norm. This was how respectable families married off their children. Even as a teenager Rahani became anxious about what was going to happen within the next ten years or less.

When Rahani was nineteen, her family immigrated to Canada. They quickly became integrated into their religious community. Rahani found work as a cashier, went to night school and was able to achieve the skills necessary to become a secretary. Whereas her home country was extremely restrictive about sex, she found Canadian society to be much more open and accepting. She came to understand what a lesbian was, and she recognized herself immediately. She sought out lesbian communities and began to loosen the fetters of guilt she had built up around her sexuality.

Shortly after her twenty-first birthday, the inevitable happened: her father informed her that he was making arrangements for her to marry a distant cousin. Her father was the patriarch of the family in the truest sense of the word. No major decision involving any family member could be taken without his prior knowledge and ultimate consent. There was virtually no room for discussion or deliberation. His word was final.

Rahani first came out to her sister, who had always been her closest confidante. Her sister embraced and kissed her, and they cried together. Her sister knew what was coming, and it was terrifying for both of them: her parents had to be informed that Rahani would not marry. As strong as her religion and culture were in her life, she knew that she could not betray her inner self, nor could she deceive everyone, especially her unsuspecting cousin.

Rahani loved her family, and the thought that she might be separated from them forever, that she would irreversibly disrupt the equilibrium within the family, was devastating to her. But what else could she do?

It suddenly occurred to Rahani that there was one option that might solve everything: suicide. She was surprised herself that this thought even entered her consciousness. She had no history of depression; in fact, she was generally happy-go-lucky, upbeat. Even though the act of suicide ran counter to the tenets of her religion and to everything she stood for, she would do what she knew she must.

Her father had left for his prayers, leaving Rahani and her mother on their own. Rahani said what she had to say and waited for a response. Her mother digested all that she heard, then uttered a wailing cry that seemed to split the room in two. She cried and cried, hardly catching a breath between wrenching sobs. Rahani went to her, offering an embrace. At first her mother rejected her touch, but soon they were both crying, holding each other, without a word. This was the scene Rahani's father saw when he returned from his prayers.

When he heard the news, he was beside himself. He slapped Rahani hard enough to draw blood. He blamed her for his anger, and accused her of being an adulteress, of besmirching their family, their religion and their god. She was no daughter of his. She must leave the house and the family.

Rahani thought she had the strength to overcome what she knew would happen. She did not. Two weeks later she was dead of an overdose of sleeping pills.

Rahani's father could show no outward expression of remorse or compassion. In his mind, any expression of grief would have raised doubts about the validity of his faith. And he was not prepared to doubt, to question. It was much easier—emotionally and psychologically—to accept that his daughter was evil and deserving of her fate than to question his religion's teachings.

Rahani's mother, too, was devout, but she opened her heart to grief, much to the displeasure of her husband. She had conceived Rahani, she had borne her for nine months and had delivered her. Rahani had been part of her body, her soul. How Rahani had come to be the way she was would be forever unknown, but she would never see her daughter as evil.

• exploring your faith

Do you view the world in a religious way? Is your culture governed by a particular scripture and your code of behavior legitimized by that scripture? Do you believe there is a god? Does your god or your scripture view homosexuality as evil, or an abomination, or unnatural, or the work of the devil? Does acceptance of your gay son or lesbian daughter imply rejection of your god and his teachings?

To answer these questions you must explore the origins of your faith to determine what edict your religion cites to justify its condemnation of homosexuality. Most people don't consider the philosophical nature of their faith, but merely accept the teachings, without question, thought, deliberation or challenge.

For much of what takes place in our daily lives, this unquestioning, accepting approach to religious faith works. But what happens if life introduces an unexpected wrinkle or a dilemma of conscience? In such cases, we are forced to understand the nature of the god in whom we believe, the meaning of the words in his scripture, and the interpretation of those words in light of new knowledge or a new perception or implication of the scriptural writings.

This is not easy for most of us. We have come to rely on others to inform us, to interpret for us, to explain to us what the scripture means, what god means. The task of religious sages throughout the millennia has been to act as our gateway to understanding scripture and the intent of the divine authority. We believe they have more insight, more knowledge, more understanding. This may well be true, but we must remember one thing: those sages were, and present-day clergy are, human beings, with wants and imperfections. All humans make mistakes, including sages. We are able to reason, we can read, we can determine whether the scripture necessarily says what our elders have said it does.

Ask yourself what kind of god you believe in. Is he a vengeful, tyrannical god or is he loving and compassionate? Is he all-powerful, all-knowing, a god who makes no errors, and hence one whose creations are perfect? Is he a god who created only heterosexuals and, if so, who was it who created homosexuals? If someone other than god created homosexuals, does this mean that there is another force in this universe capable of creating new life? Parents must ask many questions in their search for understanding.

Different religions have different answers to these and other questions, and each religious group claims to have the right answer, the only answer. But there are thousands of religions. And within each large religious group, there are sects and multiple visions of who god is, of what he teaches, of how to interpret his teachings. The great challenge for religious people is to combine scriptural teachings with independent thought and deliberation.

Generations of relatives and friends have anguished over the coming-out of a member of their family or group or tribe when homosexuality conflicts with religious beliefs. Today, some religious institutions have made proclamations about homosexuality in recognition of the fact that it has become an open reality of everyday life.

We saw what happened to Don and Rahani, the emotional and psychological turmoil that can occur when homosexuality presents itself within a deeply religious family. Both were driven to suicide by the harsh judgment they faced. There are many religious views in this world, and they often conflict with one another. Who has the truth? Whose side is God on?

Where can parents turn to help answer some of these philosophical yet very practical questions? Don's mother and

Rahani's father were quite adamant and unswerving in their conviction: trust in their faith, in their god, superseded love, compassion and sympathy for their own children. They turned to their belief, to their philosophy, but the majority of parents can not simply cast their children aside. The harshness of doing so goes against the grain in most religions.

Parents might first tell each other what their heart of hearts says is right. Then each parent could go directly to the scripture, and to the commentaries, to search for a way out of the dilemma. Must we leave scriptural interpretation to others?

Parents might go to the clergy, who might find the will and the way to assist them in using scripture to provide solace while at the same time not rejecting their child, maybe even finding a way to support the child. In the end, however, it may not be possible to find a way to reconcile religious belief and practice with a child's homosexuality. Parents might have to take action independent of the dictates of their religious group. In the Bible, Abraham was prepared to sacrifice the life of his son Isaac to his god. But God stayed Abraham's hand, sparing Isaac. Can humans do less, or must they do what the Bible says God prevented Abraham from doing and sacrifice their children on the altar of dogma?

• what the Bible says

The traditional religious tenets of the Judeo-Christian-Muslim world consider homosexuality to be an abomination. Although only male–male relations are cited, many religious authorities include female–female relations, but theological debates on this subject do occur.

The biblical source for the admonition against homosexuality is found in Leviticus 18:22: "Thou shalt not lie with a man in the manner of a woman; it is an abomination." Why would such an "abomination" appear in the Bible? In any book or commentary, the writer's biases and prejudices cannot but be present. This is as true of the writers of the Bible as it is of any book. Writers select words to convey their information and emphasis that reinforce their message. There is always a personal agenda. In the verses preceding Leviticus 18:22, the people of Israel are told not to emulate the actions of the Canaanites among whom they will live, or the actions and practices of the Egyptians whom they just left. The laws of these lands apparently allowed for same-sex marriages. In those cultures, same-sex unions were not an abomination. The writers of the Bible wanted to distinguish the Israelites from their neighbors. They achieved this in many ways, including proscribing man–man relations. One could argue, therefore, that the prohibitions of Leviticus 18:22 were motivated more by politics than by ethical-moral-spiritual standards.

To this day, religious institutions wrestle with this philosophical dilemma. The writers of Leviticus either did not understand or withheld from their readers that same-sex relationships were an established fact of life, and that homosexuals were homosexual whether or not being so was an "abomination".

This book is not a treatise on religious scholarship. But if the Bible is to be used as a basis for homophobic attitudes, then it is fair to raise questions about the intent of biblical passages. In Genesis, 18 and 19, we read of Lot, nephew of Abraham, who, while living in Sodom, was visited by three men who, unknown to Lot, were really angels of God come to assess the wickedness of Sodom. The men of Sodom heard about these visitors and demanded that Lot bring them out of the house in order to "know them" (interpreted as meaning to have homosexual intercourse). Lot tried to appease the mob by offering them his two virgin daughters to do with as they saw fit.

The interpretation of Lot's story has been the subject of much debate from many perspectives, including the feminist one. What is the message here: that male–male rape is unacceptable but male–female rape isn't? Is the message here that concern for one's male guests supersedes concern for one's daughters? How do today's religious institutions respond to the dilemma of making religious teachings consistent with the realities of life? For some it is easier than for others.

• some Christian churches

The Catholic Pastoral Centre of the Archdiocese of Toronto documents in its catechism the Catholic Church's unequivocal attitude toward homosexuality. Homosexuality is a depravity and, although homosexuals have not chosen their "condition," they can "resolutely approach Christian perfection" by choosing chastity. The text also contains the following:

> Basing itself on Sacred Scripture, which presents homosexual acts as acts of grave depravity, tradition has always declared that homosexual acts are intrinsically disordered. They are contrary to natural law. They close the sexual act to the gift of life. They do not proceed from a genuine affective and sexual complementarity. Under no circumstances can they be approved. . . .

. . . They do not choose their homosexual condition;
for most of them it is a trial. They must be accepted with
respect, compassion and sensitivity.

Homosexual persons are called to chastity. By the
virtues of self-mastery that teach them inner freedom,
at times by the support of disinterested friendship, by
prayer and sacramental grace, they can and should gradually and resolutely approach Christian perfection.

The Catholic message is clear. Homosexuality is a "condition" and homosexual acts are "intrinsically disordered" and
"of grave depravity." Redemption comes through celibacy. The
church does not leave the door open for understanding;
however, it takes the view that homosexuality has a "psychological genesis" and "remains largely unexplained."There is no
room in this view for a biological explanation for sexual orientation, whether heterosexual or homosexual.

The challenge for Catholics, and indeed for all religious
institutions, sects and governments that regard homosexuality as a "condition" that must be changed, is to recognize that
there are millions of homosexual men and women in this
world. The challenge is to reinterpret dogma and to reinvent
meanings to support the reality that homosexuality is a
natural state of some, just as heterosexuality is a natural state
of others. Through the millennia, all religions have re-writ-
ten meanings and interpretations. Otherwise we would have
only one religion with one meaning. Seeing homophobic
declarations, whether from the church, government or social
institutions, as the real aberration is a worthy and essential
goal, especially for those who believe in an all-powerful, all-

knowing, all-beneficent god who created all that exists, including homosexuals.

The Anglican Church, another Christian denomination, has a somewhat softer, less static view of homosexuality than does the Catholic Church. Further, the Anglican Church re-examines and modifies its views in response to new information and to the urgings of its membership, both straight and gay.

In 1979, the House of Bishops of the Anglican Church of Canada issued the following statement: "We believe, as Christians, that homosexual persons, as children of God, have a full and equal claim with all other persons, upon the love, acceptance, concern and pastoral care of the Church."

In addition, the bishops developed a four-point guideline for themselves when considering the admission of an individual to the church's ordained ministry.

1. Our present and future considerations about homosexuality should be pursued within the larger study of human sexuality in its totality;
2. We accept all persons, regardless of sexual orientation, as equal before God; our acceptance of persons with homosexual orientation is not an acceptance of homosexual activity;
3. We do not accept the blessing of homosexual unions;
4. We will not call into question the ordination of a person who has shared with the bishop his/her homosexual orientation if there has been a commitment to the bishop to abstain from sexual acts with persons of the same sex as part of the requirement for ordination.

This was not the end. The Anglican Church continued its deliberations not only about homosexuality, but about human sexuality in general. With respect to homosexuality, the 1995 General Synod accepted a motion that "affirmed the presence of and contributions of gay men and lesbians in the life of the church and condemned bigotry, violence and hatred directed toward any due to their sexual orientation."

The Anglican Church has not stated that homosexuality is "depravity," an "abomination," "unnatural." The homosexual is recognized as a complete and whole person. How can one Christian denomination differ so markedly from another in its view of the same issue when both base their views on the same source documents? Simple. Human beings rarely concur when interpreting images, a set of circumstances, or a set of data; each views the world in light of his or her own historical context and, however close it may be to another's, it is unique.

At its April 1997 meeting, the Anglican Church's House of Bishops continued its deliberations about the place of gays and lesbians in society and in the church. With respect to the societal status of gays and lesbians, the bishops issued the following statement:

> As Christians we believe that homosexual persons are created in the image and likeness of God and have a full and equal claim with all other persons upon the love, acceptance, concern and care of the church. As an expression of this love and care, the gospel of Jesus Christ compels Christians to oppose all forms of human injustice and to affirm that all persons are brothers and sisters for whom Christ died.

According to Anglican theology, therefore, homosexuals are equal to all other persons. If they are equal, then they are not depraved. The status of humans is determined by humans, and we can readjust our interpretations on the basis of reality, on the basis of logic and reason. The Anglican Church has opened its doors to gay and lesbian individuals in a loving communal spirit. But it has yet to go the next logical step: although the church is respectful toward homosexuals and does not find homosexuality an abomination, it cannot tolerate same-sex marriages.

The bishops were quite forthright about the differences of opinion within their House about how they should view same-sex marriages: "We disagree among ourselves whether such relationships can be expressions of God's will and purpose."

So it is, after all, humans who are going to deliberate on the meaning of divine intention. Yet again, fallible humans must make divine decisions.

There's one more piece to the Anglican story. About ordination of gays or lesbians within the church, the bishops had this to say: "We reaffirm that sexual orientation in and of itself is not a barrier to ordination or the practice of ministry within the church." Sounds reasonable, but there is catch: "At ordination, candidates promise to live their lives and shape their relationships so as to provide a 'wholesome example' to the people of God. Exemplary behaviour for persons who are not married includes a commitment to remain chaste." In other words, homosexual men and women may be ordained within the Anglican Church but may not engage in sexual activity because they are not married, and the church does not recognize homosexual marriage. The church has come a long way, but it has yet a long way still to go.

Let us take a look at yet another view of homosexual men and women, this one from the United Church of Canada. The United Church frankly admits it is searching for answers to the dilemma posed by homosexuality, but its quest involves no condemnation, no graphic labels such as "depravity" or "abomination"; there is, however, an effort to achieve human understanding of what the divine intention is in relation to human sexuality and how that intention can be honored by the church. A 1984 United Church pamphlet affirming human sexuality states the following:

7. We confess our continued confusion and struggle to understand homosexuality, even as we confess our history of sinfulness [with respect to prejudice against gay or lesbian persons in the past]
8. We confess our inability at this time, given our diversity in our understanding of the *authority* and interpretation of the Scripture, to find consensus regarding a Christian understanding of human sexuality, including homosexuality.

The United Church cannot come to a consensus about human sexuality in general, never mind homosexuality. Furthermore, the church cannot agree on the *authority* of scripture. We expect interpretation to be debated, but *authority*? Back to us fallible humans to make decisions about divine intentions.

But while the United Church expresses its doubts about philosophy and theology, it does not equivocate on the issue of homosexuals as ordained ministers. Its 1984 pamphlet contains the following council declarations:

2a. All members of Church are eligible to be considered for ordered ministry.

3. That the 32nd General Council affirm the present ordination/ commissioning procedures as outlined in the Manual, and those actions taken at the 30th General Council, which state, it is inappropriate to ask about the sexual orientation of those in the candidacy process, or those in the call/appointment/ settlement process.

• what Jewish scripture says

Just as Christian denominations differ in the approach to homosexuality, so do opinions vary within religious Judaism (a comment on Secular Humanistic Judaism follows later).

Religious Judaism covers a broad spectrum of theological ideology, from extreme ultra-orthodoxy to extreme liberalism. In North America, religious Judaism can, in general, be classified as Orthodox, Conservative, Reform or Reconstructionist, with shadings and variations in-between and at the extremes. The ultra-Orthodox view is that God wrote the Bible and handed it to the Israelites, which makes the text of the Bible God's word. The majority view, however, is that the Bible was written by men (not likely by women) who may have been divinely inspired. If men, as opposed to God, were the authors of the book, then the power and authority of the Bible can certainly be brought into question, since human fallibility is at work in it.

The Orthodox view is that the literal translation of Leviticus 18:22 holds: "Thou shalt not lie with a male in the manner

of a woman; it is an abomination." But that's not all; the Bible
calls for the death penalty if such a thing is done: "If a man lies
with a male as one lies with a woman, the two of them have
done an abhorrent thing; they shall be put to death—their
blood guilt is upon them" (Leviticus 20:13). Although men
who "lay" together were condemned to death for so doing,
there is no Jewish record that the death penalty was ever
invoked for this act.

Modern Jewish scholarship has become increasingly concil-
iatory toward and accepting of homosexuality. Many authors
have questioned the severity with which the Bible seems to treat
male homosexuality (there is no biblical commentary on
female homosexuality). What the biblical writers and their
subsequent commentators did not write about, probably didn't
even recognize or understand, was the concept of homosexual
love. What they wrote about was the homosexual act; never did
they entertain the notion that men could love men, and women
could love women, with the same depth of passion and feeling
as men and women love each other. Perhaps if they had recognized this in their own society, we would not have the destructive homophobia that is our legacy. The Israelites had to be set
apart from the people among whom they lived; condemning
the homosexual practices of these cultures was one way of
accomplishing that separation.

But one has only to turn to traditional Jewish sources to
understand that scriptures cannot be taken literally. They are
subject to study and interpretation. That is the very essence of
Judaism—to study, to learn, to interpret and reinterpret. And
it is the Orthodox Jews who spend the greatest amount of time
in study. Their mandate has been quite clearly expressed in the

Babylonian Talmud (a compilation of sixty-three volumes of commentary on the Bible based first on the oral tradition of interpretation, and ultimately codified in writing in the first 200 or 300 years of the first millennium):

> "Is not my word like fire, saith the Lord, and like a hammer which breaks the rock into pieces?" (Jeremiah 23: 29). Just as a hammer strikes the anvil and kindles clouds of sparks, so does scripture yield many meanings, as it is said: "Once did God speak, but two things have I heard" (Psalms 62:11).
>
> (Tractate Sanhedrin 34a, Babylonian Talmud)

The Bible is filled with questions and contradictions, with ambiguities. But even if the writings seem abundantly clear, one can never be certain what the meaning is. Only human beings can instill meaning and select a meaning that is consistent with logic, reason, compassion and love.

Secular Humanistic (non-religious) Jews have no trouble with this idea whatsoever. At the Conference of the Congress of Secular Jewish Organizations (a confederation of independent communities from across North America), held in Windsor, Canada, in May 1992, the following statement on sexual orientation was adopted:

> Respect for liberty governed by just laws, and the promotion of civil rights for all members of society are fundamental tenets of the philosophy of Secular Humanistic Judaism. Inherent in that liberty and those civil rights is the freedom to live in accord with one's

personal dictates and desires as long as these do not infringe on the liberties and civil rights of others. Sexual orientation, however determined, is a personal expression of one's own sexuality and a manifestation of one's own personhood and being. In a democratic society, where individual rights are paramount, no person should be deprived of dignity, self-respect and the freedom of individual self-expression on the basis of sexual orientation or any other basis within the rule of law.

It is in this spirit that the CSJO condemns discrimination against anyone because of his/her sexual orientation. To discriminate on the basis of sexual orientation contradicts the very premise upon which Secular Judaism is built.

We welcome into our ranks and into our leadership anyone whose aim it is to promote the well-being of the Secular Humanistic Jewish movement, regardless of that individual's gender or sexual orientation. In the same spirit we call upon the entire Jewish community to open its doors and its leadership to all Jews.

This is the understanding society must come to: that homosexuality is a fact of human existence and that no scripture, edict, or government decree can alter that basic fact.

It is not the individual who must change the unchangeable in order to meet the demands of religion; it is religion that must change to meet the realities of life.

Some religious groups have changed, have taken the fundamental philosophies and teachings of their religions to heart, by creating places of worship that welcome gays and lesbians. In many large cities across North America, there are churches and synagogues, either established specifically for gays and lesbians or that have an open-door policy for gays and lesbians and create special programs to incorporate them into the general community. By following such examples within their own ranks, religious institutions can begin to cast off the mantles of discrimination and rejection that have characterized so much of religious teaching for far too long.

• chapter eight

• finding acceptance

The straight world is the majority world. The world revolves
around heterosexuality in so many overt or subtle ways that
such behavior just becomes part of our everyday view of how
the world operates. Everywhere we turn we find that heterosexuality is the accepted norm. Anything that is not the "norm" is
automatically construed as "abnormal," almost by definition.
That's how we've been conditioned to think.

Government legislation defines what a family is, what a
spouse is, what inheritance rights mean, what spousal benefits
are provided under a variety of circumstances. Though the state
does not recognize homosexual marriage, the Supreme Court
of Canada stated recently that there was no good reason to treat
same-sex couples differently when it came to responsibilities
for a partner. In 1999, Ontario passed a bill extending rights and
responsibilities to same-sex couples. The general public is
coming to recognize the injustice of not treating homosexual
and heterosexual couples in a similar manner. The courts are
handing down rulings that are consistent with the Charter of
Rights. This is a beginning; much more has yet to be done.

We are surrounded by heterosexual images. Look at advertising that is so much a part of our cultural makeup. What do we see? Boy gets girl; girl gets boy. Boy entices girl; girl entices boy. We see the happy family of mother, father, children. We see masculinity represented as muscles and a woman's longing look. We see femininity represented as a svelte body and an appreciative man's stare. And what does heterosexuality sell? Everything—cars, beer, perfume, clothes. Laundry detergent is sold by a mother and father taking mud-caked sweatshirts off mud-caked children. It's all so "natural."

Some movies feature gay and lesbian characters. But what are these stories about? Their anguish, pain and struggles within a society that rejects them, victimizes them, punishes them for being who they are. Do we see movies in which gays' and lesbians' sexuality is irrelevant to the story? Not often. The gay character in that movie is usually there because of his or her gayness.

Now imagine you are a gay or lesbian living in this utterly heterosexual world. How do you feel when the world expects you to be heterosexual, to conform, to fit in? Would you deny your sexuality or express it only under very guarded circumstances? Or would you say "I am who I am and the straight world will have to accept me"? Would you say there are two separate worlds, a homosexual one and a heterosexual one? How would you feel: despondent, confident, scared, oblivious to what others said or thought? How would you tell your family? Would you tell them? How would you respond if they refused to accept the fact of your orientation? How would you integrate your partner and friends into your family activities?

And what about your school, your workplace? Could you

be yourself or would you feel you had to masquerade as a heterosexual?

Every gay and lesbian person has to face these difficult questions. Often the answers are arrived at only through great anguish.

But these questions demand answers because we all live in a society in which people view us in a particular manner and ask us questions about our life. Parents, also, must ask these questions of themselves, putting themselves into their gay children's shoes and trying to imagine what their child has to face and deal with on a daily basis. How much more prepared would you be to face some of harshness of the world if you could count on the acceptance and support of your family?

• Perry's ambition

Perry had always wanted to be a lawyer. He was a good student and took his studies seriously. In high school he played on the football team, but that was about the only extracurricular activity that he allowed himself. Although he had a circle of friends and went to the occasional party, he never went to school dances and he rarely dated. He was simply too focused on the one goal that he was determined to reach—becoming a lawyer.

At school he heard the usual boy talk, about this sexual exploit and that sexual conquest, and which girls were the easiest to coax into bed. He was also asked on innumerable occasions about his own sexual encounters and why he didn't date more often. One of his football teammates even teased him by saying: "Now, you're not going to tell me you're queer?"

This question shook him up. He had never really given much thought to sexual matters. He liked football, and he liked school, at least as a means to an end. His friend's question, which had no serious intent behind it, evoked feelings and thoughts that until then had been dormant within him. Perry suddenly woke up to the possibility that he was gay. In fact, there had been many tell-tale signs: he had a collection of he-man magazines, his erotic dreams were of men only, he once had gotten an erection in the shower room at school.

Perry went through a long painful process of understanding what homosexuality was, of accepting the fact that he was gay. When he ultimately came out to his family, he found that the world didn't collapse around him and that life went on. He was one of the lucky ones; his family was stunned, but they didn't turn from him. Their love and support didn't waver for a moment.

Perry graduated from high school with scholarships and accolades. He ultimately became a lawyer, landing a prestigious job with one of the country's largest and best-known law firms. He found himself in the middle of the international corporate world, a place he always wanted to be. He was ecstatic, but there was one thing missing, something he believed would elude him forever.

The fact that Perry was gay was known to practically every important person in his life—his family, his friends, even some of his former professors, who had recognized his brilliance and who had encouraged and counseled him in many aspects of his studies and career path. But in the one place where he wanted more than anything to be totally and completely himself, the company he worked for, he could not.

What was holding him back? No one had made any homophobic remarks. No one had told any inappropriate jokes mocking gays or lesbians. Nevertheless, his firm exuded traditional heterosexuality. Most of his colleagues were either married or had mates of the opposite sex. This was not an atmosphere that could tolerate gays and lesbians. Perry imagined scenarios in which clients, upon discovering that he was gay, immediately left his firm to find one that was more "responsible" in its hiring policies.

Perry was not alone in his belief. When he had first joined this firm, he had resolved, then and there, to keep his sexual orientation to himself. But each day that he came into work, he felt a tinge of discomfort at having created this wall around himself. He was not fully and freely himself, and he wanted to be. He turned to one of his former professors, who knew he was gay, and asked what he should do.

The professor was direct. "Perry, this is a cruel world. You had a vision of what you wanted to do in life. You've achieved that vision—it is reality. You're a success. Savour it. Don't spoil it. We live in a world of cold-hearted bastards. No one will thank you for your candor. You'll only suffer because of it."

This is what Perry had expected to hear. He maintained his silence.

• the need for acceptance

Was Perry's professor right? How much to tell and when to tell is a question gays and lesbians often face. We all want acceptance. We all want to be considered an equal partner in the various circles or circumstances in which we find ourselves. We don't want to be outsiders. Will an individual be "more equal" if colleagues know or do not know that he or she is homosexual?

What should Perry do about his discomfort at having to closet himself at his job, a job he adores and worked hard to attain? There is, of course, no easy answer, but there are some general principles. Family and friends can be a primary defense against the realities of the "cruel world" described by Perry's professor. And there is sympathetic support available beyond the world of nuclear family and friends.

Perry is way ahead of the game in the management of the adversity that his homosexuality brings. He is one of those lucky men, who has a strong buffering mechanism against the stresses of life—his family.

As strong as family support may be and as significant as it is, it is also of tremendous importance for gays and lesbians to have gay or lesbian friends, and possibly groups with whom to share fears, frustrations and dilemmas. Perry did not belong to such a group. He did not frequent community centers or other places of recreation in the homosexual community. He had never been a joiner. But he did have a significant other, the man with whom he lived and with whom he shared his frustrations, hopes and joys. He also had a coterie of male and female friends, homosexual and straight. When one of his gay friends, the editor of a local newspaper for the gay/lesbian community, urged him to come to a support group to discuss and offer help with troubling experiences, he declined. He felt the support structure he now had was all that he needed to cope with particularly stressful moments. He was silently grateful, however, that such groups existed. Just knowing there was a safe haven to which he could turn gave him a sense of peace.

But Perry was still conflicted. He sought as much help as he could. He had spoken to his professor, a man he admired and trusted, but Perry wasn't satisfied. He spoke to his parents, his siblings, his significant other; he even went to the gay support group that he had previously felt he had no need for. He heard a variety of opinions, ranging from "Tell all" to "Tell nothing." He heard stories that covered the spectrum of responses to telling all. He was still confused after all of these interventions, but he was certain about one thing: in the end, he was responsible for himself and his behaviour.

Perry envisaged every scenario he could think of. He knew he had as solid a support system as anyone could possibly want or expect. First, and foremost, he had his parents; they had time and again demonstrated their love for him and their unqualified backing for how he chose to live his life. But Perry had more: he had his siblings, his significant other, his friends both straight and gay, and, finally, a gay self-help group he knew he could turn to should he ever need them.

His deliberations covered the most optimistic outcome to the most pessimistic. What's the worse thing that could happen? They'll make it so uncomfortable for me at work that, even if they don't fire me, I'll have to leave just to preserve my sanity.

When Perry had come to the end of his deliberations, he was confident that there was only one course of action for him—he would let it be known at work that he was gay. That decision made, he now pondered how he was going to tell. The next day, he was having lunch with one of his colleagues, an eminent civil litigation lawyer, Alfred. Alfred was downcast, not his usual self. Perry recalled their conversation for me:

"Alfred, you're usually so upbeat, but you look down in the dumps today."

"Perry, my wife and I were hit with a bombshell last night. Allen, our middle son, who's twenty-two, announced to Marion and me that he was a homosexual and that he was living with a thirty-five-year-old man. Allen is home with us this week because it's reading week at school. Marion is cool and collected. I'm supposed to be the level-headed one, but I'm a basket case. I just don't know what to do or to whom to turn. Sorry about this. I didn't mean to burden you, but as smart as I'm supposed to be, I just don't know how to handle this one."

Perry's debate was over. This was not the setting in which Perry had expected to discuss his own sexual orientation, but the opportunity presented itself and he grabbed it.

By the time Perry and Alfred were finished, their one hour lunch had been extended into two and a half hours of mostly pain, anguish and tears, but it culminated in a shared sense of hope. Perry understood that he would never know if Alfred's continued closeness and support of him was rooted in a sincere indifference to Perry's homosexuality or in gratitude for the compassion and understanding Perry had shown him that enabled Alfred and Marion to understand and accept their own son's homosexuality. It was enough for him to know that, at least with Alfred, he could be himself.

One of the things that Perry thought would be of great help to Alfred and Marion was an opportunity to talk to other parents of gay and lesbian children. Perry introduced them to his own parents, who encouraged them to sympathize with and support their son.

Having told one work colleague, Perry felt confident that, little by little, everyone in his office would come to know that he was gay. Within a few months, it was general knowledge, and Perry was stunned at how irrelevant it turned out to be for the staff.

Perry couldn't believe it then, and now, thirteen years later, he still hardly believes it. He was lucky. The age of enlightenment has begun, but it is still struggling to establish itself. Every human being has the difficult task of creating a life of peace and contentment. It can be a tremendous challenge, a challenge that is lightened considerably with the support of family and friends.

• Paula and Ellie: a final commitment

Your daughter is about to get married. There's a sense of excitement in the air as you start to list all the things you have to do.

First and foremost in your mind is the fact that your daughter has found a wonderful mate for life (you hope it's for life). He's everything you could have wished for in a son-in-law. He's caring, attentive, respectful, industrious and above all, he loves your daughter with obvious joy and intensity. As an added bonus, he seems to like you, and the two of you are able to communicate rather easily.

That list: the date, the location, the clergy who will officiate, the flowers, the food, the music and, of course, the wedding attire. You shudder just a little as you think of all the work you have to do—and the expense. But the image of your beautiful daughter in her beautiful white gown, walking down the aisle and capturing the silent oohs and aahs of your invited guests, family and friends, soothes you.

You picture the church, or synagogue (with the wedding canopy under which the ceremony will take place), or the mosque, or the hall you've rented. You visualize the officiant uttering words of promise and hope for the future, maybe even mentioning the family yet to come. Joy fills your heart.

Paula's parents, too, had these fantasies when Paula was a young university student. Paula was not yet engaged, but they had met some of the young men whom she had dated and they knew that one day one of them would help fulfill their aspirations for her.

Ellie's parents had similar visions about their daughter—beautiful, intelligent, easy-going, and the object of many phone calls from many young men, all potential suitors as far as they were concerned.

Little did Paula's and Ellie's parents know that, in a few short years, plans would be under way for their fantasies to be fulfilled. There was, however, going to be one small "wrinkle" in this idyllic vision: they would be together at the ceremony at which Paula, in her gown, and Ellie, in her gown, spoke vows of commitment, not to one of those wonderful male suitors, but to each other.

Paula and Ellie's "wedding" invitation to friends and family started with the following quote:

> From every human being there rises a light that reaches straight to heaven. And when two souls that are destined to be together find each other, their streams of light flow together, and a single brighter light goes forth from their united being.

This quote came from the writings of the Baal Shem Tov (Master of the Names [of God]), born as Israel ben Eliezer in

1700. The Baal Shem Tov was a Jewish mystic who sought to go beyond the traditional stilted approach to prayer and religious practice of the Orthodox Jews. Around 1736 he revealed himself as a healer, and subsequently became the first leader of a spiritually revitalized sect of Jews known as the Chasidim (the pious ones). The quote used by Paula and Ellie is attributed to the Baal Shem Tov and would likely be in the spirit of his teachings. Never would this mystical Jewish leader in the 1700s, however, have imagined this beautiful description of two people melding their lives together being applied to same-sex marriages. As liberal as his religious thinking was in the eighteenth century, it was not enlightened about homosexual marriages.

Paula and Ellie were now both at the same point in their lives: they had made a commitment of lifelong devotion to each other and they were going to solemnize that commitment with a "marriage," a public ceremony, in which they would exchange their vows in the presence of family and friends. The experience each of them had in arriving at this point, however, was quite different.

Paula's awareness of herself as a lesbian, gained in her early twenties had been achieved through a process of "signals," as she called them. In retrospect, she recognized that she had had romantic feelings toward female friends, but these feelings were never translated into action. At age nineteen she met a woman to whom she was strongly sexually attracted, but, just when she might have started a sexual liaison with this woman, she met a man with whom she seemed to click both intellectually and emotionally. She breathed a sigh of relief, believing that, since she was happily able to date a man, she couldn't be gay. This state of what was really suspended animation lasted about a year and a half, when she ended her relationship with her male partner and established a new one with a female partner to whom she was irresistibly drawn.

She felt now that this re-emergent and unexplored side of herself could no longer be pushed aside. Her relationship with this attractive woman did not lead to sexual culmination. It was Paula's view that this woman was in denial about being a lesbian.

Paula believed that many women who are really lesbian are in denial about their homoerotic preference. In her broad experience, meeting many women under different circumstances, she came to the conclusion that many more women, beyond those who come out, are really lesbian but refuse to acknowledge it, or accept it and act upon it. Did she create this belief within herself because it was true, or because she needed justification or rationalization for her own stated sexual preference? Only someone who is unsure of herself, who lacks the courage of her conviction, would take this latter stance, and Paula didn't strike me as that sort of person.

By the time Paula had entered her second year at university, she had had her first gay sexual experience. This was much more gratifying than any heterosexual activity she had had. Any lingering doubts vanished as she explored her feelings through the many women and lesbian groups she encountered, and through the gay sex she enjoyed with increasing fervor. When Paula knew with unswerving certainty that she was gay, she was ready to come out to her parents. She described to me what it was like to tell them:

"I remember kind of warning them that I was going to tell them something that would be a bit shocking to them, that was a surprise and asking them for their support. I told them that I was dating a woman. They were actually very good. They were shocked and surprised, but not—you know. I have heard some horror stories about parents. Ellie and I could tell you lots of horror stories. They were not like that at all. It was difficult for them and it has been difficult for them. It has taken years for them to come to the comfortable place they're at now. They never rejected me as a person. They respected my honesty and my openness, though it was challenging for them. They suddenly realized it might mean my not getting married or having kids. This was a big loss for them and their dreams.

"Now my relationship is probably better than it has ever been. They have done a lot of work. They have been to a group. They have talked a lot. They love Ellie. We are accepted as a couple in the family. The ceremony was another big challenge for them. They are telling people, certain select people, that we are having a ceremony and that is a big thing. They even got to the point where they are really looking forward to it. They really moved a lot over the years."

But not all her family felt the same way. Paula had a married sister, Lesley, who had two children. Lesley was very conservative in her views about everything. Although she had come from a liberal home, she had married into a very traditional family. Her husband was loving and caring but rigid in his views about society, its politics and its mores. He was an outspoken homophobe. His joke repertoire was rife with idiotic and offensive anti–gay and anti-lesbian material. He couldn't stand to be in the presence of a gay man. When he discovered that one of his employees was gay, he made his life so miserable that the man had to resign from a job he had held for many years. There was no remorse. Gays were less than human, whether male or female.

Paula decided to tell her sister alone.

"I remember sitting in her backyard, saying that I wanted to tell her something that was really hard for me to tell and that I needed her to listen as openly as she could. I said I was in a relationship with a woman. This was a part of me that I kept hidden for a while and I was now just coming to a place of accepting this within myself. I really worked hard at staying non-reactive and pleasant, because she was very judgmental.

"She pulled out every argument in the book. 'You are screwed up.' 'You are hanging around with the wrong people.' 'You're messed up.' 'You don't know yourself.' 'Adam and Eve were man and woman and that is the way it should be. The Bible says it should be.' I did really well at the moment, staying within my own self and not losing my ground, remaining calm and not reacting and saying, 'I understand why you are like that, but you need to understand that this isn't a new thing for me. I know it's a new thing for you, but it's not new for me and I am not messed up. I actually feel happier than I ever felt in my life.' She couldn't hear that for a long time and it was very difficult for me. She was the most challenging part of the family."

Lesley gradually came to understand what Paula was trying to tell her. They both worked hard to re-establish the closeness they once knew. Paula was able to challenge Lesley on many of her prejudicial views, views she could really not support with either logic or fact. The decision to have a ceremony of commitment transformed many people, including Lesley, challenging them to enter a new level of acceptance of the gay individual. For Lesley this transformation took the form of moving from total opposition to a ceremony to understanding the reasons for it and the rationale behind it. As Paula said, "She came from a very closed, judgmental place to a warm accepting place."

Paula and Ellie do not hide the fact that they are a couple, a loving unit. At first it was difficult for Paula's family to be witness to that closeness, but they eventually accepted the sight of Paula and Ellie sitting close or touching. They have accepted them as a couple and the fact that they speak about "we" rather than "I."

Lesley's husband, Al, was another story. He and Lesley had initially been in total agreement over not showing any support for Paula. Her behavior, they thought, was wrong, vile, reprehensible. There was no way they could support her because to do so would be to condone her actions.

Lesley, however, did not have it in her heart to "divorce" Paula, her only sibling. She spoke with her parents and was shocked to discover how quickly they were coming to grips with this new reality in their lives. She was surprised that they wanted to understand. They wanted to help; Paula, after all, was their daughter.

When Lesley observed her parents' response, a wave of shame and regret came over her. She understood the intense bond of love that her parents had for their children. She had always taken it for granted before, but now she saw its intensity, its meaning. Her parents accepted Paula; could she do less?

Lesley began to talk to Paula, coldly and from a distance at first. Paula tried to explain; she brought Lesley reading material; she introduced Lesley to Ellie. Lesley didn't know what to expect before meeting her. But when she met an attractive, intelligent woman who had an interesting life, who could engage her in conversation, Lesley came to view her, not as some ogre who had misled her sister, but a person with whom she could have a civilized relationship.

As Lesley began to understand and accept her sister more and more, she felt she could introduce the topic to Al. Paula was going to have a ceremony of commitment. Lesley felt she should be there, and she wanted Al and the children to attend. It wouldn't be accurate to say that Al underwent a transformation. His homophobia ran deep. But Al did have a sense of family and he understood that his absence would be painful to Lesley and to his in-laws. Reluctantly he allowed himself to speak to Paula; he was even civil to Ellie. He would come to the ceremony for the sake of the family cohesion, not because he condoned it in any way.

Ellie had first had sexual relations with a woman when she was sixteen. She'd had many partners, most of them female, but also occasionally males. When Ellie was a teenager, she really did not understand what it meant to be "lesbian," but many of her female partners helped her recognize her own feelings. Ellie was very open to accepting herself completely. She didn't go through the process of interpreting "signals" as Paula had done.

Ellie put it this way: "If you cannot bring yourself to become intimate with yourself, then what is it all about? I just totally said that obviously this is who I am and that is the stage at which I came out."

Ellie was surprised by the difficulties Paula had in the process of coming out since her own family was so accepting. She told her parents separately and recalled for me their response.

"My dad was like, 'Tell me something I don't already know.'

My mother, although suspicious, was still very affected and more emotional and more like, 'What did I do and are you certain? Is there any hope?' and all that kind of stuff.

"My father isn't a typical parent. Having a kind of open and honest conversation with his kids brought so much joy to him that he just felt blessed that I was sharing this with him. He is not judgmental. My family was always very open about sex, even when I was being brought up. There were lots of parties and lots of craziness going on, and we were always free to ask whatever questions we wanted to ask and they would always answer honestly. My grade 5 teacher was concerned because she thought that, at age ten, I knew too much.

"Of course, my mother was a little hesitant at the beginning, but now it's great, it's wonderful, and she is loving and support-ive. We have a very close relationship. I know that she still has issues. If I were to say, 'Mom, guess what, you're not going to believe this, but I met a man and I am in love and this is who I want to be with,' she would be, 'Wow!' She loves Paula and she wants me to be happy and all of those kind of things, but I know that she has her own wishes and I have to challenge her on them."

• a ceremony of commitment

Both Paula and Ellie were in relationships when they met, but they soon fell deeply in love. Paula recalled how the idea of a ceremony of commitment grew:

"I had gone through an extremely stressful period involving my work and my studies. It took me a year to recover physically and emotionally, and I felt as if Ellie took care of the fort. She took care of me emotionally. She took care of food. She took care of everything at that time, and supported me immensely, and I felt a responsibility to give something back. I knew that Ellie had this childhood dream of getting married. It was never something that was part of my growing up. I knew that it was important for her and that it was a dream, a dream in which I could share. That's how it started. So I created a very beautiful evening for us. We had gone out for dinner and then we went back to the park, where we had a very strong experience when we first met, a very strong experience that made us feel that we had to be together. I brought a basket with some champagne and wine glasses and a sarong that I laid out, and a book on meditation for couples and, underneath, these bracelets that I had bought for us. Ellie asked me if I would marry her."

Ellie added: "At first we just kind of told our family, and then we spent the next four months or so working through the family issues. It was about standing up for who we are. We were very adamant about acceptance and standing up for our rights as a couple, and that we love each other no differently than any two people who love each other, and why are we not as deserving of a ceremony as any two people who love each other and want to form a life together?"

The ceremony was planned in great detail. The location, of course, had to be a public venue. No house of worship would have tolerated a same-sex marriage. The officiant had to be someone special, someone with an extremely liberal view of what a "marriage" means and the depth of feeling that Paula and Ellie felt toward each other. The intensity of this feeling was more important to the officiant than the fact that this was not a traditional male–female marriage sanctioned by the civil authorities. Of course, the invitations, the food, the entertainment, all the details had to be tended to.

The most difficult hurdle to overcome was dealing with the responses of those who were to be invited—family members and friends. Nuclear-family members who knew Paula and Ellie were gay were not too surprised when they learned that a ceremony of commitment was planned. This was also true of their closest straight friends, who had long since ceased being surprised by how Paula and Ellie had put their lives together. The greatest difficulty they encountered was from members of the extended family and from friends of their parents and siblings.

One woman was absolutely shocked that Paula and Ellie would not only want to make a public display of their homosexual love for each other but also try to use the "sacred tradition" of marriage to do so. She was incensed at the thought of such an event and at the idea that there would be guests there who, by their very presence, would be condoning such an "unnatural" act. She refused to come.

This woman, Martha, had two straight children. One of them, Mark, was a health-care worker in a hospice where he had the opportunity to provide comfort and aid to a variety people from different social, ethnic and religious backgrounds. He had come to understand what empathy really meant—what hardship, grief and alienation really cost. He had come to understand that concern for his fellow humans was of greater importance than the culture or sexual orientation of the clients with whom he dealt.

When he heard of his mother's reaction to receiving a "wedding" invitation from Paula and Ellie, he tried to intervene.

Mark had a two-year-old daughter, Suzie, whom Martha described as the "jewel" of her life.

Mark challenged her with a hypothetical situation. Suzie was only two years old now and, of course, it was not possible to know what her sexual orientation would be. It could well be homosexual. What would Martha think then? Would Suzie still be the "jewel" of her life? Would she go to her "marriage" ceremony if she was uniting with another woman?

Martha told Mark this whole conversation was too much for her and she brought it to a close. But Mark's question haunted her. Could Suzie turn out to be a lesbian? How would that be possible in this loving family into which she had been born and from which she would be internalizing so many values?

But what if it did happen? Would she go to the ceremony? How could she not go? It was her granddaughter whom she would love forever; of course, she would go.

Martha called Ellie and apologized for the delay in responding to the invitation. She said she would be honored to come.

Paula and Ellie had spent the previous three years creating a solid base to their relationship, building roots and defining themselves as a couple. Together they had built hopes and dreams for the future and had determined where they wanted to go as a couple. The building blocks for a life together had been put into place. They were both ready for a ceremony of commitment.

Their "wedding" did not have the sanction of civil law, but it was in the style of a traditional wedding, with their own innovative twist. The officiant had worked with them to compose the vows and to ensure that the right atmosphere was created. A good friend of theirs, a singer, provided the musical portion of the ceremony. All the people who counted in their lives were there—parents, siblings, family and friends. Paula and Ellie had accepted each other, and they had expended considerable effort to help those close to them accept them both as individuals and as a couple. Was there skepticism in the minds of some of the guests? Of course. How many gay weddings had they attended? It was a new idea, but a very sensible step for two people who had expressed not only love for each other, but the desire to spend the rest of their lives together.

Although the two sets of parents initially had some reservations about a "wedding," they came to the point of not only accepting it, but feeling a sense of elation in seeing their children so joyous over the event and over their union.

Long-term monogamous relationships are not the exclusive property of heterosexual couples. Many homosexuals, like many heterosexuals, seek the comfort and security of one partner, one home, and the sharing of a life exclusively with a loved one.

Both individually and as a couple, Paula and Ellie had experienced something we all strive for as we enter into the various projects of our lives: acceptance. They were not naive enough to believe that everyone who came to the ceremony accepted all that they heard and saw without reservation. But in what situation is there total acceptance by all participants? This might occur in a religious context, but not generally in the activities of everyday life. By accepting an invitation to attend the ceremony, the attendees had either accepted the idea of a same-sex marriage or were at least showing respect for how Paula and Ellie had planned their lives together.

• the gift of acceptance

Perry had found acceptance of the person he was in his home, among his family. He wanted to freely be that same person in the workplace. When he finally opened up at work and found that, except for his renewed sense of self, life did not really change, he felt a refreshing sense of serenity.

The acceptance of parents is the most significant positive force that encourages us to proceed, particularly when we have a close relationship with our parents. Perry, Paula and Ellie all ultimately had their parents' support in the major enterprises of their lives. This is a powerful part of creating self-confidence and the courage to undertake the challenges that life flings at us.

The path to the point of total acceptance may be a hard road to travel for many parents, relatives and friends of gays and lesbians. But to reach this goal not only lifts the great burden of loneliness and alienation from the gay child, but also frees the parents, relatives and friends from a negative attitude and from the constant, but vain, hope that the child will somehow become what he or she is not and cannot become.

Coming to the point of acceptance is an evolutionary process. It's not something that anyone can reasonably expect to happen overnight, but it is something that one *can* reasonably expect to happen. Here are a few suggestions for ways that parents and others can begin to acquaint themselves with what it means to be a gay or lesbian in a predominantly heterosexual and often hostile world.

There are many books to read on the subject of homosexuality, written from many different perspectives. There are academic books and popular books; books by gays and lesbians and books by parents. It is not possible to list the thousands of volumes that have been written on the subject, but I have selected a few for inclusion in the bibliography. If you live in a large urban center, there may well be one or more bookshops that focus on gay and lesbian issues. The proprietors of such shops will be more than happy to give you specific suggestions. Many movies deal with gay and lesbian experiences. Most of these will be available for rental from your local video store. You can gather a list of such movies by asking at bookstores or at gay and lesbian centers in your community.

Your child can be a great source of knowledge and can help you understand what his or her sexual feelings mean and what it's like to live with a homoerotic preference. Learning through your child can be enhanced if you do some reading and investigation of your own. Maybe there are a few things that you can help your child understand.

What you initially hear from your child may seem strange, foreign. You may experience a form of culture shock, and you may find the truth hard to absorb initially. It would be reasonable to discuss your feelings, your shock, with trusted friends, with gay people you know, or with a counselor who can help you deal with this newfound knowledge. Such counseling could include both parents, the gay or lesbian child, other children. The purpose of the counseling would not be to try to "convert" the gay or lesbian child to heterosexuality but to help family members understand and accept his or her homosexuality.

Parents, families and friends of gays or lesbians do not themselves have to enter into the gay world as a prerequisite for offering acceptance. The important point is to have some degree of understanding of the world. This, in turn, will provide insights into the child and the kind of environment he or she identifies with.

Parents should rightly be concerned about their children, but that concern should honestly focus on the child and not on the parent. Concern for the child should not be manipulative and really mean: "Change your orientation. It's bad for you, and I don't like it." Such concern is self-directed, not for your child. Be honest with yourself first.

Your child may already have a partner or may have one at some time in the future. Be open to this possibility. Be prepared to meet the partner, and do not judge him or her on the basis of his or her sexual orientation.

Parents can help themselves and their children by working toward acceptance and by engaging other family members and friends, and the community at large, in the exercise of acceptance. This is a moment to show strength. You're the most valuable support system your child could have.

• chapter nine

• conclusion—for now

Why are we bothered by what other people do, how they look, how they dress? Why is being judgmental so integrated into our social fabric? We tend to criticize others at every turn, eager to find fault. It is so easy never to question our biases, our prejudices, but simply to accept the most simplistic and primitive of human beliefs: that there is one right way and a myriad of wrong ways to live. Any other perspective would put us into a state of anarchy, of uncertainty; it would force us to form our own opinions and, to do that we might have to stand alone, which causes anxiety, insecurity, the sense of being an outsider. And how many have the self-confidence to be an outsider? We seek communities of people with whom we can be insiders. That is one reason we accept the common "wisdom," even though it may be corrupt and simply wrong.

When I was a senior trainee in medicine, years ago, I recall a well-respected cardiologist, a bright, energetic and intelligent woman, the head of the service I was on at the time, berating the newest member of our team, not for medical inadequacy, since he was one of the brightest trainees around, but for his long hair and his thick black beard (this was at a time when long hair and thick beards were not the style of the day). Her conservative belief that doctors had to look a certain way was deeply ingrained. Presumably she was open to new ideas in medicine, to a new understanding of diseases of the heart, an area in which new information was appearing faster than text-books could be printed.

Prejudices of one sort or another occupy major portions of our life. Some of our institutions pass along those prejudices inherent in them. Many religions, for example, advocate love and compassion for one's fellow human beings, while others state dogmatically, with conviction, that our way is the right way, and any other way is an express lane to eternal damnation. Sometimes, paradoxically, the doctrines of love and damnation coexist within the same religion. All theistic religions have, by definition, an inherent bias built into them, a bias that proclaims "My god is the true god, and my religious practices can, therefore, be nothing but the way of truth." The history of the world is replete with the tragic consequences of carrying this belief to its extremes.

In this book, I have tried to encourage you as parents, family and friends of gay and lesbian young people to re-evaluate your belief systems, your prejudices, your perceptions of life in general, and your perceptions and views of homosexuality in particular. There is no one who does not have a homosexual friend, colleague, acquaintance or family member. Apart from their erotic preference, there is nothing that distinguishes homosexuals as a group from heterosexuals. Why do we insist on putting them into categories, into kinds or types of human beings, simply on the basis of their sexual preference? We don't do this with heterosexuals. We judge the heterosexual world on the basis of deeds, not the propensity to have sex with a member of the opposite sex. If it offends us, we may condemn promiscuity, adultery or group sex among heterosexuals, but we don't condemn the heterosexuality, where the same behavior occurs. Some might say we condemn homosexuality because the homosexual is not like us, and, if you're not like us, if you're different, then you're something less than us. History provides many examples of such attitudes. To Adolf Hitler for example, Jews were different; therefore, they were the enemy and had to be destroyed. Hitler felt the same about other groups, such as homosexuals and Gypsies; so they, too, had to be destroyed. This is an extreme example of prejudice, to be sure, but extremes grow out of the irrational prejudices of a few.

It has been said by many that the basis of homophobia is the fear among heterosexuals that they will become homosexual, or the fear that the seeds of homosexuality live within us all. Until there is irrefutable evidence that this view is accurate, no one can say that there is any basis to such an allegation. Prejudice can work both ways, and we must be sensitive to that fact.

The underlying philosophy presented in this book is that we all are free, that freedom is part of the human condition. We are born with this freedom, as we are born to think, to digest food, to have sexual feelings. We all possess the freedom to make choices, to make decisions, wherever we live on this earth, and in whatever state (as long as we are mentally competent). We may live in an open society that promotes democracy; we may live under coercive and repressive conditions; yet no one can take away our innate freedom to make choices. We choose how we respond to the world around us. Similarly, we choose how we respond to the discovery that someone we love or know is gay or lesbian.

You as parents don't have to be fearful of, or condemnatory of, or aghast at the idea that a child of yours or of anyone you know is gay or lesbian. The simple fact of our innate freedom is that I am myself and you are yourself; I am not you, and you are not me. I am responsible for myself and I can choose for myself.

Consider this: despite our innate freedom, no one chooses his or her sexual orientation. We all can choose the kind of sexual behavior in which we wish to engage, but we have no choice in our sexual orientation, our erotic preference.

We don't know how sexual preference develops. It is simply there. Despite the theories of how homosexual preference may occur, described earlier in this book, it is completely irrelevant how we came to have our erotic preference—whether by active choice or by some other biological or experiential event.

If you consider your prejudices honestly, you will find no evidence of a rational element in them. Most are rooted in misunderstanding, misinformation and a desire to enjoy the comfort of the status quo, of being embraced by others who share a belief in the mythology that fostered and bolsters your prejudice.

I look forward to the day when there is no longer a need for a book like this. That will be the day when sexual orientation will be totally irrelevant. That will be the day when the multiple meanings of "family" and of "spouse" will be a recognized fact of life—in practice and in law. That will be the day when all the heterosexual clichés of daily life will no longer be a part of our culture, when we don't take for granted that the word "couple" means a man and a woman, when we don't take for granted that "marriage" implies a union between a man and a woman, when "spousal" benefits accrue to the spouse regardless of his or her sex.

Until such a day arrives, books of this nature will have to be written. Parents, families and friends of gays and lesbians will have to be given encouragement to go against the tide of society, to change societal attitudes, to change laws, in order to find for themselves and bestow on others personal happiness and acceptance.

• Canadian resources

There are hundreds if not thousands of resource centers or facilities for gays and lesbians in Canada. Parents can easily tap into these resources; simply consulting your children and their friends will likely lead you to most of the information you'll need. Go to the library, and look for gay and lesbian bookstores, newspapers, periodicals. See movies featuring gay and lesbian issues. Explore the Internet. Not every piece of information you find will be useful, or reliable, or will offer answers to all your questions, but if you read enough, if you talk to as many informed people as you can, you'll begin to expand your knowledge, your understanding and your ability to accept. One contact can lead to another. If you put forth an honest effort to gain information, you won't have any problem finding it.

There are two books that are extremely helpful guides to sources of information:

1. *Canada's Gay Guide, 1999/2000 Edition*
   (issued annually), edited by Trevor Jacques.
   Published by Click and Drag, Inc.
   P.O. Box 1591-607

55 Bloor Street West
Toronto, ON M4Y 1R8
Tel: (416) 962-1040
Fax: (416) 962-1044

2. *Gayellow Pages, USA and Canada* (National Edition
   No. 23), 1999/2000.
   Published by Renaissance House
   P.O. Box 533, Village Station
   New York, New York 10014-0533
   Tel: (212) 674-0120
   Fax: (212) 420-1126

In Toronto, I was given considerable assistance in obtaining the titles of a variety of materials by the staff of

Glad Day Bookshop
Gay and Lesbian Literature
598A Yonge Street
Toronto, ON M4Y 1Z3
Tel: (416) 961-4161
Fax: (416) 961-1624

Parents, their children and friends will find within the list of Canadian groups below specific resources and organizations that can provide education, information and support. How did I arrive at this particular list? In a completely arbitrary manner—hence there will be omissions, since I could not have included every credible contact. My motive in compiling this list was to provide a broad overview of groups that would be of particular benefit to parents of gay and lesbian children.

If an organization listed below does not quite fit the bill, or does not adequately deal with your particular need, it may still be worth contacting as you could be directed to precisely the right source for you.

Western Canada

1 First United Church Gay and Lesbian Support Group
   320 East Hastings Street
   Vancouver, British Columbia V6A 1P4
   Tel: (604) 681-8365

2 Quaker Lesbian & Gay People & Their Supporters
   Box 321
   1525 Robson Street
   Vancouver, British Columbia V6G 1L3
   Tel: (604) 683-4176

3 Gay & Lesbian Community Centre of Edmonton (GLCCE)
   P.O. Box 1852
   Edmonton, Alberta T5J 2P2
   Tel: (780) 488-3234 or (780) 482-2855 (events line)
   Fax: (780) 482-2855
   E-mail: glcce@freenet.edmonton.ab.ca
   Web: http://www.freenet.edmonton.ab.ca/glcce

4 Gay & Lesbian Community Services Association (GLCSA)
   Suite 206, 223 12th Avenue
   Calgary, Alberta T2R 0G9
   Tel: (403) 234-8973
   (403) 234-9752

5 Gay Community of Regina
   P.O. Box 3414
   Regina, Saskatchewan S4P 3J8
   Tel: (306) 522-7343

6 St. Matthias The Apostle Mission
   P.O. Box 33079
   Regina, Saskatchewan S4T 7X2
   Tel: (306) 569-7452
   E-mail: aa497@gpfn.sk.ca
   Web: http://www.netministries.org/see/churches/ch04614

7 West Central Saskatchewan Support & Education
P.O. Box 326
Lashburn, Saskatchewan S0M 1H0
Tel: (306) 285-3667

8 The Canadian Gay, Lesbian & Bi Resource Directory
386 Montrose Street
Winnipeg, Manitoba R3M 3M8
Tel: (800) 245-2734
(204) 488-1805
E-mail: kc@cglbdrd.com
Web: http://www.gaycanada.com

9 Metropolitan Community Church of Winnipeg (MCCW)
Box 2601, 116 Sherbrooke Street
Winnipeg, Manitoba R3G 4K9
Tel: (204) 774-5354
E-mail: mccwpg@icenter.net

10 Chutzpah—Lesbian and Gay Jewish Group
P.O. Box 1661
Winnipeg, Manitoba R3C 2Z6

11 First Unitarian Universalist Church of Winnipeg
790 Banning Street
Winnipeg, Manitoba R3E 2H9
Tel: (204) 786-6797

Ontario

1 AIDS Committee of Toronto (ACT)
4th Floor
399 Church Street
Toronto, Ontario M5B 2J6
Tel: (416) 340-2437
(416) 340-8844 (hotline)
E-mail: ask@actoronto.org
Web: http://www.actoronto.org

2 Amnesty International Lesbian, Gay, Transgendered
  & Bisexual Group
  p.o. Box 74
  552 Church Street
  Toronto, Ontario M4Y 2E3
  Tel: (416) 927-1453
  E-mail: relliott@netrover.com

3 Armed Services Lambda Association (ASLA)
  Tel: (613) 236-9587
  E-mail: ArmedServices@gaycanada.com
  Web: http://www.gaycanada.com/armedservices

4 Asian Gay & Lesbian Phone Support Services (ALPSS)
  Suite 107
  33 Isabella Street
  Toronto, Ontario M4Y 2P7
  Tel: (416) 920-2577
  E-mail: keanoo@geocities.com
  Web: http://www.geocities.com/Tokyo/4550/got.htm

5 Association of Lesbians & Gays of Ottawa
  p.o. Box 7046
  250 Durocher Street
  Vanier, Ontario K1L 5A0
  Tel: (613) 741-2374
  E-mail: Sylmar@cyberus.com

6 Brethren/Mennonite Council for Lesbian & Gay Concerns –
  Ontario
  Tel: (519) 579-3394
  Fax: (416) 489-9425

7 Congregation Keshet Shalom
  Tel: (416) 925-1408
  (416) 925-9872 Ext. 2073

8 First Unitarian Church of Hamilton
  170 Dundurn Street South
  Hamilton, Ontario L8P 4K3
  Tel: (905) 527-8441
  Fax: (905) 527-6420

9 Gay & Lesbian Parents Coalition International
p.o. Box 187, Station F
Toronto, Ontario M4Y 2L5

10 Homophile Association of London Ontario (HALO)
649 Colborne Street
London, Ontario N6A 3Z2
Tel: (519) 433-3551
(519) 433-3762
Fax: (519) 433-7129
Web: http://www2.gaycanada.com/halo

11 Jewish Support Group for Families of Gays & Lesbians
c/o Holy Blossom Temple
1950 Bathurst Street
Toronto, Ontario M5P 3K9
Tel: (416) 763-9111

12 Kingston Lesbian, Gay, Bisexual, Transidentified Association
51 Queen's Crescent
Kingston, Ontario K7L 3N6
Tel: (613) 533-2960
Fax: (613) 533-2712

13 The Lesbian Gay Bi Youth Line
p.o. Box 62, Station F
Toronto, Ontario M4Y 2L4
Tel: (800) 268-9688
(416) 962-9688
E-mail: lgbline@icomm.ca
Web: http://www.icomm.ca/lgbline

14 Metropolitan Community Church of Toronto (MCCT)
115 Simpson Avenue
Toronto, Ontario M4K 1A1
Tel: (416) 406-6228
Fax: (416) 466-5207
E-mail: info@MCCToronto.com
Web: http://www.MCCToronto.com

15 The Old Catholic Church
  R.R. #1
  Midland, Ontario L4R 4K3
  Tel: (705) 835-6940
  E-mail: burch@web.net

16 Rainbow Metropolitan Community Church (MCC) –
  Guelph
  c/o Saint Mathias Anglican Church
  171 Kortright Road West
  Guelph, Ontario N1G 3N9
  Tel: (519) 822-6451

17 Saint Anthony Catholic Prayer Group
  P.O. Box 66
  552 Church Street
  Toronto, Ontario M4Y 2E3
  Tel: (416) 966-0598

18 Southern Ontario Gay & Lesbian Association of Doctors
  (SOGLAD)
  P.O. Box 1022, Station F
  Toronto, Ontario M4Y 2T7
  Tel: (416) 515-8096
  E-mail: soglad@web.net
  Web: http://www.web.net/~soglad

19 Timmins & Area Lesbians & Gays Association (TALGA)
  P.O. Box 2175
  Timmins, Ontario P4N 7X8
  Tel: (705) 360-0689
  (705) 268-8254
  Fax: (705) 268-3332
  E-mail: talg@nt.net
  Web: http://www.gaycanada.com/talga

20 Toronto Association for Gay/Lesbian Arts, Recreation, &
  Culture (TAGLARC)
  92 Gloucester Street
  Toronto, Ontario M4Y 1L9
  Tel: (416) 960-9788
  E-mail: TAGLARC@attcanada.net

21 Trent Lesbian & Gay Collective (TLGC)
   Suite 4, Jung House,
   290 Rubidge Street
   Peterborough, Ontario K9J 3P4
   Tel: (705) 743-5414

22 2-Spirited People of 1st Nations (TPFN)
   4th Floor, 14 College Street
   Toronto, Ontario M4Y 1S2
   Tel: (416) 944-9300
   Fax: (416) 944-8381
   E-mail: spirit@aracnet.net

23 University of Western Ontario Research Facility for Gay and
   Lesbian Studies
   Room 355, University College
   London, Ontario N6A 3K7
   Tel: (519) 661-2111 Ext. 5828
   E-mail: pridelib@julian.uwo.ca
   Web: http://www.uwa.ca/pridelib.html

Quebec

1 L'Androgyne Bookstore
   3636 boulevard Saint Laurent
   Montreal, Quebec H2X 2V4
   Tel: (514) 842-4765
   E-mail: libandro@aol.com
   Web: http://www.kiosque.com/pub/andro

2 Centre Communautaire des Gais et Lesbiennes de Montreal
   (CCGLM)
   C.P. 476, Succursale C
   Montreal, Quebec H2L 4K4
   Tel: (514) 528-8424
   Fax: (514) 528-9708
   E-mail: info@ccglm.qc.ca
   Web: http://www.ccglm.qc.ca

3 Comité des Lesbiennes & des Gais du Conseil Central de
   Montreal – CSN
   Tel: (514) 596-7092

4 Eglise Communautaire du Village
   Suite 2
   1320 boulevard de Maisonneuve est
   Montreal, Quebec H2L 2A5
   Tel: (514) 528-9574
   E-mail: eglise.village@sympatico.ca
   Web: http://www.odyssee.net/~prince/eglise.html

5 Gai Écoute
   C.P. 1006, Succursale C
   Montreal, Quebec H2L 4V2
   Tel: (800) 505-1010
   Fax: (514) 866-8157
   E-mail: courrier@gai-ecoute.qc.ca
   Web: http://www.gai-ecoute.qc.ca

6 Groupe de Parents d'Enfants Gais du Saguenay
   Tel: (418) 690-9109
   Fax: (418) 541-6882

7 Groupe de Parents Gais & Lesbiennes
   C.P. 66008
   620 rue Saint-Jean
   Quebec, Quebec G1R 5T1
   Tel: (418) 641-2572

8 Gruppo Italiano Gay e Lesbico di Montreal
   C.P. 476, Succursale C
   Montreal, Quebec H2L 4K4
   Tel: (514) 528-8424
   E-mail: aerogram@odyssee.net
   Web: http://home.rogerswave.ca/wysiwyg/italian.htm

9 Parents d'Enfants Gai(e)s/Enfants de Parents Gai(e)s
   CLSC Thérèse-de-Blainville
   55 rue Saint-Joseph
   Sainte-Thérèse, Quebec J7E 4Y5
   Tel: (450) 979-3427

10 Projet Jeunesse Idem
Suite 003
109 rue Wright
Hull, Quebec J8X 2G7
Tel: (819) 776-2727
(613) 237-9872 Ext. 2012
Fax: (819) 776-2001
E-mail: bras@cactuscom.com
Web: http://www.geocities.com/WestHollywood/1453

11 Regroupement des Gais & Lesbiennes de la Region du
Kamouraska, Rivière-du-Loup, Témiscouata
Tel: (418) 862-8978

12 Regroupement des Gais & Lesbiennes de l'Est du Quebec
C.P. 31
Rimouski, Quebec G5L 7B7
Tel: (418) 722-4012

Eastern Canada

1 Affirm United
P.O. Box 33067
Halifax, Nova Scotia B3L 4T6
Tel: (902) 461-4528
E-mail: stewarar@gov.ns.ca

2 The Cape Breton Gay & Lesbian Equality Project
P.O. Box 745
Sydney, Nova Scotia B1P 6H7
Tel: (902) 567-1766
E-mail: CBGLEP@hotmail.com

3 Equality for Gays & Lesbians Everywhere (EGALE)
Nova Scotia
Tel: (902) 827-3969
E-mail: kim@egale.ca
Web: http://www.egale.ca

4 Halifax Pride Committee
P.O. Box 36018
Halifax, Nova Scotia B3J 3S9
Tel: (902) 422-2274
E-mail: Pride@chebucto.ns.ca
Web: http://www.chebucto.ns.ca/CommunitySupport/HPC

5 Safe Harbour Metropolitan Community Church
(MCC)-Halifax
Universalist Unitarian Church
5500 Inglis Street
Halifax, Nova Scotia B3H 1J8
Tel: (902) 453-9249
E-mail: Dyoung@sprint.ca
Web: http://www.geocities.com/WestHollywood/4037

6 Bisexual, Gay, & Lesbian Association for Support (BGLAS)
P.O. Box 20002
Corner Brook, Newfoundland A2H 7J5

7 Gay/Lesbian/Bisexual Support & Information Line
P.O. Box 6221
Saint John's, Newfoundland A1C 6J9
Tel: (709) 753-4297

8 Newfoundland Gays & Lesbians for Equality, Inc. (NGALE)
P.O. Box 6221
Saint John's, Newfoundland A1C 6J9
Tel: (709) 753-4297
E-mail: NGALE@geocities.com
Web: http://www.geocities.com/WestHollywood/4291

Northern Canada

Gay/Lesbian Alliance of the Yukon Territory
P.O. Box 5604
Whitehorse, Yukon Y1A 5H4
Tel: (413) 667-7857

Parents, Families, & Friends of Lesbians, Gays, Bisexuals & Transgenders (PFLAG)

British Columbia

PFLAG Comox Valley BC
259B Archery Crescent
Courtenay, BC V9N 8Y1
Laurel Walton (250) 334-8015
E-mail: atippett@bc.sympatico.ca

PFLAG Prince George BC
5635 Moriarty Crescent
Prince George, BC V2N 3P7
Carole Tkachuk (250) 964-6753

PFLAG Vancouver BC
8602 Granville Street
P.O. Box 30075
Vancouver, BC V6P 5A0
Betty Ewing (604) 689-3711
Fax: (604) 263-0378
E-mail: betew@intergate.bc.ca

PFLAG Victoria BC
P.O. Box 5474, Station B
Victoria, BC V8R 6S4
Elizabeth McLaughlin (250) 385-9462
Fax: (250) 642-7743
E-mail: pflag@gayvictoria.com
Web: http://www.PFLAG Victoria BC

Alberta

PFLAG Calgary AB
6620 Bowness Road NW,
Calgary, AB T3B 0G1
Deb Bridge, (403) 286-4094
E-mail: pflag@canuck.com
or Gail & Dave, 3312 Centre B Street, NW
Calgary, AB T2K 0V6
(403) 277-5227
E-mail: gallen@cadvision.com

PFLAG /T Edmonton AB
P.O. Box 1852, Suite 103
10612-124 Street
Edmonton, AB T5N 1S4
Lynne (780) 462-5958
E-mail: pflag@freenet.edmonton.ab.ca
Web: http://www.PFLAG/T Edmonton. AB

Saskatchewan

PFLAG Saskatoon SK
2802 Calder Avenue
Saskatoon, SK S7J 1W1
Myrna Rolfes (306) 343-7315 or Dennis (306) 664-4228
or Jean (306) 477-l476
E-mail: rolfes@duke.usask.ca

Manitoba

PFLAG Winnipeg MB
#1003 - 100 Adamar Road
Winnipeg, MB R3T 3X6
Audrey Wheatland (204) 275-0799

Ontario

PFLAG Belleville ON
RR 1,
Corbyville, ON K0K 1V0
Winifred Perryman (613) 968-3881

PFLAG Brampton/Mississauga ON
35 Willis Drive
Brampton, ON L6W LB2
Mary Jones (905) 457-4570
E-mail: ljones@pathcom.com

Cambridge (not a chapter, for contact only)
Mary (519)650-6155

PFLAG Cornwall ON
1040 East Route 800
St. Albert, ON K0A 3C0
Denise Latulippe 1 (888) 886-4715 or (613) 987-1640

PFLAG Peterborough/Fenelon Falls ON
c/o Carol Milroy
RR#1
Fenelon Falls, ON K0M 1N0
Tel: (705) 887-6830

PFLAG Guelph,Kitchener/Waterloo ON
c/o GLOBE
P.O. Box 273, CSA
University of Guelph,
Guelph, ON N1G 2W1
Kitchener Grace & Bill: (519) 822-6912, Evie (519) 742-0700 ;
Cambridge Sue: (519) 650-6155

PFLAG Hamilton–Wentworth ON
45 Glen Cannon Drive
Stoney Creek, ON L8G 2Z6

Irene or Jack Taylor (905) 662-1510
E-mail: taylori@cgocable.net

PFLAG Kingston ON
P.O. Box 1751
Kingston, ON K7L 5J6
Marion Marks (613) 546-0267

PFLAG London ON
#125-2230 Trafalgar Street
London, ON N5V 4J9
Diana Van Weeren (519) 451-2697 or Brian (519) 457-0640
E-mail: briand1@execulink.com

PFLAG Simcoe County ON
Box 23, RR#1
Midland, ON L4R 4K3
Kay Pollock (705) 534-3275

PFLAG North Bay ON
569 Elmwood Avenue
North Bay, ON P1B 8X8
Kathy Andrew (705) 476-6274
or Gays, Lesbians & Bisexuals of North Bay
(705) 495-4545
E-mail: andrew@efni.com

PFLAG Oakville ON
144 Burnet Street
Oakville, ON L6K 1C2
Anne Marie Read (905) 849-5686
E-mail: wallyr@sympatico.ca

PFLAG Ottawa ON
381 Lefebvre Way
Orleans, ON K1E 2W5
Diana & Dennis Stimson (613) 834-9880
or Gayline (613) 238-1717 (7pm–10pm)
E-mail: tbarnes@conductor.synapse.net
or stimson@direct-internet.net

PFLAG Grey–Bruce (Counties) ON
Linda or Murray 1 (800) 821-7714
or Owen Sound Health Unit 1 (800) 263-3456 ext 320
E-mail: lin.ron@bmts.com

PFLAG Peterborough
Tel: (705) 748-3405
E-mail: pflagpeterboro@yahoo.com

PFLAG Sarnia-Bluewater ON
P.O. Box 2635
Sarnia ON N7T 7V8
Chatham: Mary-Jo & Jim (519) 542-8343
Petrolia: Richard & Eileen (519) 352-7038
Pt Huron, US: Brenda (519) 882-4554;
Roberta and John (810) 987-7527
E-mail: jim.callaghan@lambton.on.ca

PFLAG Haldimand–Norfolk County ON
c/o Haldimand–Norfolk Regional Health Dept. P.O. Box 247
12 Gilbertson Drive
Simcoe, ON N3Y 4L1
Wendy Holmes (519) 426-6170 ext 234
or Jayne Holmes ext. 225
E-mail: HNpfflag@aol.com

PFLAG St. Catharines ON
P.O. Box 28032 Lakeport P.O.
600 Ontario Street
St. Catharines, ON L2N 7P8
Monica Davis (905) 934-9933
E-mail: jdmack@netcom.ca

PFLAG Toronto ON
115 Simpson Avenue
Toronto, ON M4K 1A1
Marg Nosworthy (416) 406-6378

Fax: (416) 406-1727
E-mail: toronto@pflag.ca
Web: http://www.PFLAG Toronto ON

PFLAG Toronto East ON
Suite 200, 1200 Markham Road
Toronto, ON M1H 3C3
Marlene Morais (416) 264-4606
Fax: (416) 264-0127;
E-mail: toronto_east@pflag.ca
or marlene@pflag.ca
or Ruby Hamilton (416) 483-1845
E-mail: Ruby_Hamilton@sbe.scarborough.on.ca
Web: http://www.PFLAG Toronto East ON

PFLAG York Region ON
1 James Foxway
Toronto, ON M2K 2S2
Marilyn Byers (416) 225-2232
E-mail: marilynp@idirect.com

PFLAG Windsor ON
1168 Drouillard Road, Ste B
Windsor, ON N8Y 2R1
Mary Lou & Ernie Hamelin (519) 973-7671

Quebec

PFLAG Montreal, Quebec
12A rue Radcliffe
Montréal Ouest
H4X 1B9
Pat Cannon (514) 488-4608

New Brunswick

PFLAG Fredericton NB
P.O. Box 1556, Station A
Fredericton, NB E3B 5G2
Francis (506) 454-8349

PFLAG Moncton NB
35 Union Street
Sackville, NB E4L 4M6
Eldon Hay (506) 536-0599
E-mail: erhay@mta.ca

PFLAG Saint John NB
274 Germain Street
Saint John, NB E2L 2G8
Judith Meinert (506) 652-3995

PFLAG Woodstock/Carleton County NB
Richard Blaquiere
119 Jules Drive
Woodstock, NB E7M 1Z2
Tel: (506) 328-4868
E-mail: richardb@nbnet.nb.ca
also Sherri Drake (506) 328-0910

Nova Scotia

PFLAG Amherst NS
RR #1
Southampton, NS B0M 1W0
Muriel Goodwin (902) 546-2344
E-mail: erhay@mta.ca

PFLAG Halifax NS
159 Hebridean Drive
Herring Cove, NS B3V 1H4
Don & Sylvia Sullivan (902) 479-1856
or Jan Morrell (902) 454-6903
or Ron Garnett-Doucette (902) 443-3747

PFLAG Pictou County NS
509 Mountain Road
New Glasgow, NS B2H 3X4
Ellen Ryan (902) 752-3596

PFLAG Annapolis Valley (Wolfville)
NS 1034 Highland Avenue
New Minas, NS B4N 3J5
Joan & Fred (902) 681-3622

• bibliography

This bibliography is, of necessity, incomplete. There's just so much literature available from so many perspectives. The references listed have been included because they are either sources for some of the scientific discussion or sources that broadly cover the dilemmas and questions faced by gay and lesbian individuals, their parents, family and friends.

Bookstores that focus on gay and lesbian issues will be able to help you find other relevant materials.

Aarons, Leroy. *Prayers for Bobby—A Mother's Coming to Terms with the Suicide of Her Gay Son.* San Francisco: Harper San Francisco, 1995.

Alter, H.J. "Descartes before the Horse: I Clone, Therefore I Am: The Hepatitis C Virus in Current Perspective." *Annals of Internal Medicine* 115/8 (October 15, 1991): 644–49.

Bailey, J.M., and R.C. Pillard. "A Genetic Study of Male Sexual Orientation." *Archives of General Psychiatry* 48 (1991): 1089–96.

Bass, Ellen, and Kate Kaufman. *Free Your Mind: The Book for Gay, Lesbian, and Bisexual Youth—and Their Allies.* New York: Harper-Perennial / HarperCollins, 1996.

Bernstein, Robert A. *Straight Parents, Gay Children: Keeping Families Together.* New York: Thunder's Month Press, 1995.

Bodsworth, N.J.; P. Cunningham, J. Kaldor, and B. Donovan. "Hepatitis C Virus Infection in a Large Cohort of Homosexually Active Men: Independent Associations with HIV-1 Infection and Injecting Drug Use but Not Sexual Behaviour." *Genitourinary Medicine,* 72/2 (April 1996): 118–22.

Borhek, Mary V. *My Son Eric: A Mother's Struggle to Accept Her Gay Son and Discover Herself.* Cleveland: Pilgrim Press, 1979.

Bozzette, S.A., S.H. Berry, N. Duan, et al. "The Care of HIV-infected Adults in the United States." *The New England Journal of Medicine,* 339/26 (December 24,1998): 1897–1904.

Deschenes, M. "New Developments in Viral Hepatitis." *The Canadian Journal of CME,* January 1999: 101–10.

Duberman, Martin, ed. *A Queer World: The Center for Gay and Lesbian Studies Reader.* New York: New York University Press, 1997.

Fairchild, Betty, and Nancy Hayward. *Now That You Know—A Parents' Guide to Understanding Their Gay and Lesbian Children.* San Diego: Harcourt Brace, 1998.

Fanta, Marlene, and Christopher Shyer. *Not Like Other Boys—Growing Up Gay: A Mother & Son Look Back.* Boston: Houghton Mifflin, 1996.

Griffin, Carolyn Welch, Wirth, Marian S., Wirth, Arthur G. *Beyond Acceptance – Parents of Lesbians and Gays Talk about Their Experiences.* New York: St. Martin's, 1996.

Haase, A.T., and T.W. Schacker. "Potential for the Transmission of HIV-1 Despite Highly Active Antiretroviral Therapy." *The New England Journal of Medicine* 339/25 (December 17, 1998): 1846–48.

Hankins, Catherine. "AIDS: What Is Happening with Women?" *The Canadian Journal of CME,* July 1995, 37–42.

Heathcote, E.J. "Hepatitis C: A Growing Problem." *Parkhurst Exchange,* September 1998, 72–76.

Kaffko, Karen. "Life Stress, Self-disclosure and Family Support: A Study of Lesbian and Gay Men's Perceptions of Their Families." Thesis for Doctor of Education, University of Toronto, 1993.

Langevin, Ron. *Sexual Strands*. Hillsdale, NJ: Lawrence Erlbaum Associates, 1983.

Lee, W.M. "Hepatitis B Virus Infection: Medical Progress." *New England Journal of Medicine* 337/24 (December 11, 1997): 1733–45.

LeVay, Simon. "A Difference in Hypothalamic Structure between Heterosexual and Homosexual Men." *Science* 253 (1991): 1034–37.

Marcus, Eric. *Is It a Choice?—Answers to 300 of the Most Frequently Asked Questions About Gay & Lesbian People*. San Francisco: Harper San Francisco, 1999.

McDougall, Bryce (Ed.). *My Child Is Gay—How Parents React When They Hear the News*. London: Allen & Unwin, 1998.

Ndimbie, O.K., L.A. Kingsley, S. Nedjar, and C.R. Rinaldo. "Hepatitis C Virus Infection in Male Homosexual Cohort: Risk Factor Analysis." *Genitourinary Medicine* 72(3) (June 1996): 213–16.

Powers, Bob, and Alan Ellis. *A Family and Friend's Guide to Sexual Orientation*. New York: Routledge, 1996.

Radkowsky, M., and L.J. Siegel. "The Gay Adolescent: Stressors, Adaptations, and Psychosocial Interventions." *Clinical Psychological Review*. 17(2) (1997): 191–216.

Sanders, Michael, Jerald Bain, and Ron Langevin. "Feminine Gender Identity in Homosexual Men: How Common Is It?" In R. Langevin (Ed.). *Erotic Preference, Gender Identity, and Aggression in Men: New Research Studies*, pp. 249–59. Hillsdale, NJ: Lawrence Erlbaum Associates, 1985.

————"Peripheral Sex Hormones, Homosexuality, and Gender Identity." In R. Langevin (Ed.), *Erotic Preference, Gender Identity, and Aggression in Men: New Research Studies*. pp 227–47. Hillsdale NJ: Lawrence Erlbaum Associates, 1985.

Sherman, M. "Hepatitis C: What You and Your Patient Should Know." *Canadian Journal of CME*, October 1995: 47–59.

Steinbrook, Robert. "Caring for People with Human Immunodeficiency Virus Infection." *New England Journal of Medicine* 330/26
(December 24, 1998): 1926–28.

Ward, J.W., and J.S. Duchin. "The Epidemiology of HIV and AIDS
in the United States." *AIDS Clinical Review*, 1997–98: 1–45.

White, J.C. "HIV Risk Assessment and Prevention in Lesbians and
Women Who Have Sex with Women: Practical Information for
Clinicans." *Health Care Women International*: 18/2 (March/April
1997): 127–38.

Zhang, H., G. Dornadula, M. Beumont, L. Livornese Jr., B. Van
Uitert, K. Henning, R.J. Pomerantz, "Human Immunodeficiency
Virus Type I in the Semen of Men Receiving Highly Active Antiretroviral Therapy." *New England Journal of Medicine*, (December
17, 1998): 1803–09.

• index

Abraham and Isaac, biblical story of, 126

Acceptance of homosexuality
as permanent, 17, 61–69, 98, 99–102, 166
at work, personal story, 141–147
importance of, 30–33, 139–162
in same-sex marriage, personal story, 147–159

Acquired immune deficiency syndrome. See AIDS

AIDS, 52–56
relationship to HIV, 53–54

Anglican Church
and same-sex marriages, 132
conditional ordination of homosexual clergy, 130, 133
position on homosexuality, 130–132

Bailey, J.M., 97–98

Bain, Dr. Jerald, 60, 95, 108–109, 111

Behavioral role vs. gender identity, 108, 111

Bible, statement on homosexuality, 126–128

Bibliography, 189–192

Biological theories on cause of homosexuality, 93–99

Books on homosexuality, 189–192

Catholic Church, position on homosexuality, 128–130

Causes of homosexuality, theories, 91–113
aversion to women (in men), 106
biological, 93–99
disturbed relationship with parents (in men), 111–112
environmental, 102–105
genetic (in men), 97–99
hormonal (in men), 93–95
hypothalamus size (in men), 95–97
learning theory (in men), 112–113
male partners as surrogate women (in men), 107
narcissism (in men), 107
psychosocial, 105–113

strong female gender identity (in men), 107–111

Changes of attitude in families, 27–44

Christian Churches. See Churches, positions on homosexuality

Chromosomes, 62–63, 64
influence on behavior, 63

Churches, positions on homosexuality, 128–134. See also Judaism, positions on homosexuality
Anglican, 130–132
Catholic, 128–130
United Church of Canada, 133–134

Clergy, homosexual, ordination of
in Anglican Church, 130, 133
in United Church of Canada, 133–134

Coming out to family
importance of, 32–36
personal stories, 11, 13–14, 21–23, 42–44, 81–86, 119–121, 122–123
responses, 9–26

Concerns of families of homosexuals, 27

Counseling, value and purpose of, 10–11, 21, 65, 84

Cross-dressing, 58–59

Cultural conditioning, power of, 87–88

Cultural expectations and living one's own life, 71–90

Destructive family reactions to child's homosexuality, 14, 15–16, 83–86, 121–123

Diseases, supportive actions by families to help prevent AIDS and hepatitis, 57. See also AIDS; Hepatitis

Environment as cause of homosexuality, 102
as assumed by family, personal story, 104–105

Expectations, parental and cultural, 71–90

Families
ability to change, 27–44

acceptance of child's homosexuality, importance of, 30–33, 139–162
connectedness, value of, 30–33
definition, 9
disturbed relationships as cause of homosexuality in men, 111–112
expectations and child living own life, 71–90
factors they need to consider, 18–20
lack of control over child's sexual orientation, 17
religious, and need to explore religious tenets, 123–126
strength based on externals, 17
strength, internal, 30–33
support from, importance of, 12, 19, 26, 30–33
supportive actions to help prevent AIDS and hepatitis, 57
variations in, 9
Family history as cause of homosexuality, 102, 104–105
Family responses to child's homosexuality, 9–26
negative, 12–16, 35–36, 104–105, 121–123
positive, 11–12, 20–26, 28–30, 83–86, 117–121
Fear of coming out to family, 32, 81–82, 119, 122
Femininity
as culturally, not genetically, determined, 69
in gay men, 59–61
stereotypical, 67–69
Freedom of choice, 165–166
as a right, 73
meaning of, 88–89
Freund, Dr. Kurt, 60
Gay. See entries beginning with Homosexual; Homosexuality
Gender identity, 60–61
and transsexualism, 108–111
female, as cause of homosexuality in men, 107–111
personal story, 109–110
scale, 60

vs. gender role, 108, 111
Genetic determination of sex, 62–63
Genetic makeup of humans, 62–63
Genetic theory on cause of homosexuality, 97–98
HBC (hepatitis C virus), 56, 57
HBV (hepatitis B virus), 56, 57
Hepatitis
and homosexual men and women, myth, 56–57
B and C viruses, 56, 57
transmission of, 56
Heterosexual nature of the world and the need for acceptance, 139–162
HIV, 53–55
prevention, 54–55
relationship to AIDS, 53–54
transmission, 54
Homophobia, 37–38
antidotes to, 38–39
entrenched in religions, 117–138
in parents, personal stories, 37, 39–44, 84–86
official, in Catholic Church, 128–130
Homosexual men
and AIDS, myth, 52–56
and pedophilia, myth, 50–52
and transvestitism, myth, 58–59
not sole recipients of HIV, 55–56
Homosexual men and women
and AIDS, 52–56
and hepatitis, 56–57
mannerisms, myth, 59–61
Homosexuality
as an illness, 50
impossibility of changing, 17, 61–69, 98, 99–102, 166
myths and misconceptions about, 47–70
Homosexuality, theoretical causes, 48–50, 91–113
aversion to women (in men), 106
biological, 93–99
disturbed relationship with parents (in men), 111–112
environmental, 102–105
genetic (in men), 97–99

hormones (in men), 93–95
hypothalamus size (in men), 95–97
learning theory (in men), 112–113
male partners as surrogate women
(in men), 107
narcissism (in men), 107
psychosocial, 105–113
strong female gender identity (in
men), 107–111
Hormonal theory of cause of homosexuality, 93–95
Human immunodeficiency virus. See
HIV
Hypothalamus, 94
small size as cause of homosexuality
in men, 95–97
Information, sources of, 169–187
Information-gathering, value of,
28–30, 38–39, 160–161
Isolation of not communicating
homosexuality to family, 32–36
Judaism, positions on homosexuality,
134–137
Orthodox, 134–136
Secular Humanistic, 136–137
Kaffko, Karen, 32–33
Klinefelter's syndrome, 64–65
Langevin, Dr. Ron, 60, 95, 108–109, 111
Learning-theory cause of homosexu-
ality, 112–113
Lesbian. See entries beginning with
Homosexual; Homosexuality
LeVay, Simon, 96–97
Leviticus 18:22, 127
Lot, biblical story of, 127–128
Maleness vs. masculinity, 66–67
Marriage, same-sex
and Anglican Church, 132
personal story, 147–159
Masculinity, 65–67
culturally determined, not genetic,
69
difficulty of defining, 63–65, 67
in lesbians, 59–60
vs. maleness, 66–67
Misconceptions about homosexuality,
47–70

Myths
about homosexuality, 47–70
cultural, 71–90
Narcissism as cause of homosexuality
in men, 107
Negative family responses to child's
homosexuality, 36–37, 83–86,
104–105, 121–123
Ordination of homosexual clergy
in Anglican Church, 130, 133
in United Church of Canada,
133–134
Organizations, gay and lesbian, Canadian, contact information, 171–179
Parents. See Families; entries beginning with Family
Parents, Families and Friends of
Lesbians, Gays, Bisexuals and
Transgenders (PFLAG), 29–30
chapters across Canada, contact
information, 180–187
Pedophilia, 51–52
and homosexual men, 52
Personal stories
acceptance in work environment,
141–147
acknowledgement of own homosexuality, 99–102
environmental causes of homosexuality assumed by family, 104–105
family responses to child's homosexuality, negative, 12–16, 36–37,
83–86, 104–105, 121–123
family responses to child's homosexuality, positive, 10–12, 20–26,
28–30, 117–121
marriage, same-sex, 147–159
misconceptions about homosexuality, 47–50
need to come out, 33–36
parental change of attitude, 39–44
religion and family response to
child's homosexuality, 14–16,
117–123
sexual confusion, 77–81
sexual orientation as unchangeable,
99–102

transsexualism, 109–110
PFLAG, 29–30
  chapters across Canada, contact
    information, 180–187
Pillard, R.C., 97–98
Positive family reactions to child's
  homosexuality, 11–12, 23–26, 28–30,
  83, 117–121
Prejudice, 37–38, 89–90, 163–165
Psychosocial theories of cause of
  homosexuality, 105–113
Reading material, 189–192
Religion. See also Churches, positions
  on homosexuality; Judaism, positions on homosexuality
  and family responses to child's
    homosexuality, 15–16, 117–123
  homophobic attitudes in, 117–138
Religious families and the need to
  explore religious tenets, 123–126
Religious groups that welcome
  lesbians and gay men, 137–138
Religious writings
  need for reinterpretation, 124, 126,
    129–130, 135–136
  personal and cultural agendas in,
    125, 127–128
Resources, 169–187
Rigid family reaction to child's homosexuality, 15–16, 17
Role, behavioral, vs. gender identity,
  108, 111
Sanders, Dr. Michael, 60, 95, 108–109,
  111
Sartre, Jean-Paul, 88
Secular Humanistic Judaism, position
  on homosexuality, 136–137
Self, real, finding it and living it, 71–90
Sexual orientation
  impossibility of changing, 17, 61–69,
    98, 99–102, 166
  impossibility of changing, personal
    story, 99–102
  no family control over, 17
  possibility of changing, myth, 61–69
Sexuality, female, arising from
  outdated stereotype, 68

Sources of information, 169–187
Support groups for families and
  friends of lesbians and gay men
  contact information for PFLAG
    chapters across Canada, 180–187
  value of, 27, 29–30
Supportive families, value of, 12, 19,
  26, 30–33
Testosterone
  behavioral effects, 94–95
  level as possible cause of homosex-
    uality, 95
Transgenderism. See Transsexualism
Transsexualism
  and homosexuality, 108–111
  and transvestitism, 59
  personal story, 109–110
Transvestitism
  and gay men, myth, 58–59
  in transsexuals, 59
Twin studies in search for genetic
  factors as cause of homosexuality,
  97–98
Uniqueness of each person, regardless
  of culturally determined gender
  role, 70
United Church of Canada
  lack of consensus on homosexual-
    ity, 133–134
  ordination of homosexual clergy,
    133–134
Women
  anxiety about, as cause of homosex-
    uality in men, 107
  aversion to, as cause of homosexu-
    ality in men, 106
Work, acceptance at, personal story,
  141–147